P9-CJZ-041

THE RED MEAT SURVIVORS

ANOLA & CLEVON DIXON © LINDA DUFURRENA

Some of ranching's old-timers admit to ignoring the problems of cholesterol and other unnamed and often unsubstantiated handicaps. They believe that red meat is good, which is proven here, simply by age and attitude.

Published by Purple Coyote Corp. & RANGE magazine

Produced and edited by C.J. Hadley

© LINDA DUFURRENA

One of the pioneer trails across northern Nevada stuck close to the Humboldt River until all water disappeared into a sink just west of the current town of Lovelock. At this point, the immigrants were about 90 miles east of the mighty Sierra Nevada. It would be many days until they crossed the Black Rock Desert on the Applegate Trail en route to Oregon or reached the Truckee Meadows, like the Donner Party, en route to California.

Publisher/Editor: C.J. Hadley
Designer: John Bardwell
Senior Writer: Tim Findley
Photographers: Larry Angier, Linda Dufurrena
Editorial Assistant: Ann Galli
Staff: Joey Hall, Joyce Smith
Proofreader: Denyse Pellettieri White

Library of Congress Cataloging-in-Publication Data
Hadley, C.J.
THE RED MEAT SURVIVORS
Caroline Joy Hadley
ISBN 978-0-9744563-7-9
LCCN 2010934449

Publication of this book was made possible by generous donations from people who care about the American West.

Published by Purple Coyote Corp. & RANGE magazine, Carson City, Nevada, with assistance from the Nevada Rangeland Resources Commission.

$26 U.S.A.
Printed in China

A century of memories

Listening to the old people. By C.J. Hadley

This book shares a glimpse of life since the late 1800s, memories of rough, tough times of ranchers who took care of land while raising cattle and sheep. It is an almost forgotten era of close families living with valued horses and dogs, because, out there isolated and alone, they had to depend on each other.

Producing food for the nation is not an easy life, but most cowboys and sheepherders admit they wouldn't change a thing, even though their stories follow the trail of boom and bust through two world wars and the Great Depression.

The people who lived through those times are now old, wise, experienced, realistic, imaginative, innovative. They are our greatest teachers, with a work ethic, a self-reliance and strength of character that should be emulated.

When we met Claire O'Rourke, she was helping senior citizens with their tax returns. She was 108, still living alone. At a century, Jerry Rajnus was, with gusto, sharing his book, "My First 100 Years." And Dave Grove, 98, was burning the weeds in his ditches as a reporter arrived. He cooked her breakfast, made coffee, talked ranch history, gave an animated tour of barns, corrals and workshops on the home place that was settled in the 1890s, and then picked watercress from his creek to fix her a fresh, green lunch.

There are cowboys and Indians within these pages, and hopeful Bascos and other immigrants seeking a better life. Some of the pioneers are descendants of Sacajawea, some knew Pancho Villa, others lived through the 1906 San Francisco Earthquake, and a few even met Pretty Boy Floyd.

In the early days they lived in tents, shacks, sheep wagons and on covered buckboards. Many just threw a bedroll or blanket out in the sage and used a saddle for a pillow. But as soon as they could, and to improve their lives, they built homes of more substantial rock, sod or wood.

These stories come from the pages of *RANGE* magazine over the past twenty years. Some of the stars are gone, but many carry on, with the same strength, determination, and love of family that always held them together. But not one has forgotten the times when they were tested.

When Dorcas Lowery's mother got sick, her father took her to Dove Creek to the doctor. "I was ten, alone for a week with horses and cows to feed and water, hogs and chickens to care for," Dorcas says. "I had to milk the cows and cut wood for the stove. I wasn't late one time for school. Now they call the cops if you leave a ten-year-old alone."

Scarcity and hardship were constant companions, as was Mother Nature. She challenged with flood, drought, pestilence, fire, oppressive heat, biting cold and snow so deep it killed. But you will also find that despite tragedy and agony, humor helped get them through the worst times.

Listen to the old people. Learn from their stories. Feel their love for life and country and, if you are lucky, snatch a little bit of their vigor.

© LARRY ANGIER

John James with, from left, Della Lefty, Dottie Lefty and Brieanna Swett. They are at the annual chestnut roast at the Milligan School near Clinton, California. Each year, on the Saturday after Thanksgiving, family and friends of the ranching Cuneo family gather for food, friendship and freshly roasted chestnuts. Several generations attend. John's ancestors came to California from France around Cape Horn in the 1840s to ranch in pre-U.S. California.

Mountains are nature's art, repainted each night into dawn by the blend of forests and streams, shadows and light that is never quite the same as you saw at sunset. Sometimes when you watch from a peak, it seems you can see all of the mountains that form the backbone of our nation and almost imagine all the mysteries and riches that they seclude. But it is only an illusion forming another horizon, and the truth we most often miss in that inspiration is that no matter how much you see and count as many mountains, you cannot see the one you are standing on.

HENRY MOUNTAINS AT DUSK, UTAH. PHOTO © LARRY ANGIER

Contents

Tribute to our Forebears

Penny for a pound. By Tim Findley

History is one thing. Personal experience is another. The vital accounts of events produced in books or documentaries provide us with an inspiring record of our past and our times. But the exceptional personal memories told knee to knee on an easy country evening establish the texture of the great fabric of life in the United States. The true story of liberty and freedom that the world recognizes as uniquely "American" is really a tapestry of individual success and failure, courage and fear that can be understood in the mind, but also felt in the heart. One size or one description does not fit us all, even today, and that is what makes our culture and our character so rich.

The collected stories in this book provide a path through the American West in the memories of those who continue to make it a place like no other in the world. There are landmarks in events and interests and even changes to the language that will be familiar to all, and each is best told by those who lived it so well.

It isn't so easy as waiting for Grandpa to settle down after dinner or supper into a comfortable old chair, with two or three generations of kids around him waiting their next rightful chance to share a piece of his lap and the family dogs circling around their tails a couple of times before finding their spots by the fire. It's never so simple to see a hierarchy of close country relations assembling in such anticipation. But as visitors from *RANGE* magazine we've seen it many times and, beyond that, heard from more than we can remember that they were sure Norman Rockwell used their families as models for his paintings in *The Saturday Evening Post*.

Grandpa wasn't necessarily the smartest man in the county, but he'd usually agree that he was among the most experienced. Men who manage retail stores or run big factories all have that kind of authority. But if Grandpa was a rancher, it meant that he had land, and as he often reminded his family, earned from that "a penny for a pound." So a family gathering was bound to begin like a business meeting, depending on the issues they all understood. If things were going perfectly well on the ranch, which they never did, the old man might cock an eye around the room saying, "Let's have a little good news for a change." You hated to throw that "A" in algebra away so easily, so to save it for a slightly more humble moment you could always comment on the blessings of good weather.

Nobody's grandfather in the history of America has ever survived a full lifetime without encountering the consarned worst episode of bad weather ever known to man. Your grandfather lived through the coldest, deepest blizzards, most murderous tornadoes, and longest throat-shrinking droughts that would have left all the children in the room shivering helpless waifs. If the snow in grandpa's time ever reached up to his chest, he remembered tunneling through it every year just to reach his classroom. You lucky kids just can't imagine...

And so, again, would begin Weather 101 in the tales that were only exaggerated by succeeding tellers. Yarns were always the best. A trip to the rodeo twenty years back, the long night to save a colt's life in the barn, the time your sister disappeared and was thought to have been kidnapped until she was found sleeping in an upstairs bedroom.

Even today, it is not so surprising to find a family ranch where a couple in their 80s celebrate more than a half-century of marriage still engaged in the important parts of life. Often, Grandma would follow up on Grandpa's talk with a rendition of her own best news—which she always seemed to hear first. Usually, another of the younger ones would have a ball of yarn over each thumb as Grandma spun it into one big ball that would become somebody's winter sweater.

Grandmothers and mothers are marvelous at the transitions from bad news to better. The story of a really big blizzard always leaves room for the memory of a bright, warming blaze in the fireplace, and they are very good at keeping track of such things. They always know who the giggles are from when the latest of the little ones have been rolled down the neck of the mare into a haystack. Those cupcakes after dinner always get the credit they deserve, and those algebra high marks are just as remarkable as somebody's new poem. Sometimes, even today, mothers and grandmothers are especially authoritative on such subjects because they are themselves the teachers. Their success has been shown most recently in the current generation of college kids with remarkable success from being homeschooled.

The kids will always have their say, not so much because somebody tells them to, but because it becomes so hard after a while not to burst out with something just they know—that big frog on the pond, or the incredible shape on a fallen leaf, some scary thump they heard last night, or how much Grandpa snores.

If everybody seems to be doing something on their own, like fixing that broken bridle again or browsing through the family album, even if it seems sometimes they all must be talking at once, it will find its own point of culmination when somebody has fallen asleep in a lap or a dog is chasing a rabbit through its dream.

When trouble comes, as they all know it will, the family knows instinctively how much they must pull together. Crop prices fail for reasons not foreseen, a drought stretches into another summer. The old man knows about this; he has given them the perseverance to make it part of their chores in just staying together. It always worked out in those old tales and usually with some humor at the end that they might even look forward to. But other, bigger troubles and tragedies were certain to be known. The time would come when a son or a daughter must be sent off to

© LARRY ANGIER

The Cuneo ranching family celebrates Independence Day at Blue Creek Canyon in the Stanislaus National Forest in Northern California. This is Evelyn Cuneo with nine of her twelve great-grandchildren.

military service or college, maybe never to come back. It was an intensely personal sense of loss not shared in the same way by each of them, but it was also felt for what it was as the loss of a limb leaving a hole in the sky.

Family gatherings don't really have agendas, and nobody will be taking notes. There will be no minutes. But there will be memories impossible to find anywhere else. Technology has changed them through many lifetimes since new gadgets on the tractor became impossible for Grandpa to describe and radio and television have brought about new rules of good behavior. It's hard to imagine the same anticipation among a row of kids with their elbows holding up their chins before a 50-inch high-definition TV. Indeed, the family itself has been changed by the demand of technology.

But American culture has evolved through such changes before, facing challenges far beyond their fences, meeting new ideas that, surprisingly, have emerged from just such confidence to solve a problem or to build on something good to make it better. And even as the world seems so dramatically to be changing again, those fundamental lessons we learned best in the love of each other are still to many Americans their most valuable heritage. Maybe the ranch or the farm is gone and maybe even the pressure of a new civilization moving upon us makes us wish we could have it all back.

But it was always meant to be a memory and a little moral compass we each could understand. Can't buy that, and it doesn't seem right that folks would try to sell it as something you can own without knowing. It's there still in recalling the pride Grandpa had for hard work. "Penny for a pound," he used to say. "Penny for a pound."

It is a scene of sweet science that only nature could portray. Cattle grazing on a pastoral slope in the warmth of another season that changes with the motion of earth, never quite the same, yet always reassuring in the great cycle of life.

CATTLE GRAZE IN RICH, DEEP GRASS NEAR CAMANCHE RESERVOIR IN NORTHERN CALIFORNIA. PHOTO © LARRY ANGIER

TEXAS . SPRING 1997

Annie Lou Gowens White, 88

A quilt out of 'baccy sacks.

Annie Lou Gowens White ain't what you would call a wilting lily. She ranches the hardest country this side of the moon. We are talking unmerciful country: the Texas badlands between the Pecos and Rio Grande rivers. She's tended Angora goats and Rambouillet sheep on the vast, wild Chihuahua Desert through 69 years of summer's furnace heat and winter's whistling blue northers. Vigorous, confident and sparkling at 88, Annie's been through it all: droughts, floods, good markets and bad markets.

It all started in 1929. Annie Lou lived in Del Rio, Texas, attending school at Draughton's Business College. She caught a young rancher's eye, and he came "a-calling" at her home. At the start, Annie Lou wasn't real interested in the wrangler, Andy John Wesley White, but consented to go to a silent picture show with him at the Texas Theater. The courtship quickly flowered, especially in Andy's heart, and he proposed. Annie Lou's mamma wanted her to marry a city fellow, not a rancher, so she turned him down. Andy was hit pretty hard by this, and told her he was joining the Army. Annie Lou backtracked, and said, "No you ain't! We are gittin' married!"

"It cost me $3 to git married, and it was worth every cent!"

And so they eloped and were married by the justice of the peace at his home in Del Rio. "It cost me $3 to git married," Annie Lou says, "and it was worth every cent!"

Annie Lou packed a few clothes, then she and Andy lit out for the Pecos Ranch in his Model-T Ford pickup. She says her new in-laws, Wes and Maudie White, were "struck near speechless when Andy and me come rolling in. They didn't have any idea we was a-fixin' to git married and we never had time or money for a honeymoon—we went to ranching sheep and goats. We were so poor, I saved Andy's Bull Durham 'baccy sacks and thread from feed sacks to make a quilt for our bed."

Wes and Maudie White came to the Pecos in 1909 from New Mexico. They worked as sheepherders, living in a tent while raising the children and saving money for their own spread. Andy went to school in Langtry, Pandale and Sanderson, Texas, in those years of following the flocks. He was packed off to the wooden sidewalks and dirt streets of Del Rio to get a proper education, but came home with a wife.

"It was a shock to have skunks and snakes come up to tell me good morning," Annie Lou says, "but I loved every minute of ranch life." Andy gave her a gentle jenny to use until she learned to ride a horse. She tamed a bevy of doves that rode on her shoulders as she went about her chores.

Annie Lou and Andy worked hard, bought their own ranch, expanded their flocks and bought more land. Shoulder to shoulder, they fought floods, poverty and drought. For years, they lived long miles from neighbors and towns at the end of a rough dirt road. Together they hewed home, and a living, from the thorny outback.

"We lived a hard life," she says, "but it was healthful. We had a good garden, fruit trees, and plenty of sheep, goats, cows and venison to eat. Ha! I still eat as much durn meat as my false teeth will allow."

Andy took the long, final ride in 1994, so today Annie Lou lives on her Lozier Canyon Ranch near Dryden, Texas, with daughter Lou and son-in-law John Smith. She spends long hours on their pleasant porch, gazing over the ranch, watching her grandchildren and great-grandchildren work the land as she and Andy did for more than six decades. Her eyes moisten with past memories, then she sparks a smile. "I run away from the city and married that cowboy, and I ain't regretted a dang minute of it!"—*J. Zane Walley*

PHOTOS COURTESY WHITE FAMILY

ABOVE: Annie Lou at home in Del Rio on her 35th birthday. LEFT: At age five with parents Lou Edith and Andy. AT TOP: Annie Lou today.

Jerry Rajnus, 101

Shot and killed but still alive.

Jerry Rajnus has been many things, but first and foremost he's a farmer. He's had many years to pursue a variety of interests. He's well into trying something different, living his second century.

It's been an active life for Jerry, who turned 100 on June 7, 2007, and celebrated his milestone at a large family reunion in the southern Oregon town of Malin, where he lived most of his life. Jerry was born in Baltimore, Maryland, in 1907, but moved to Malin with his family in 1913.

"My mind is as clear as a bell. I live by myself. I do the gardening. I do the cooking. I wash my clothes, I take my pills," says Jerry, who lives in a mobile home in Roseburg, near his daughter and son-in-law Jean and Tom Ridenour.

"He's as sharp as a tack. He just can't hear or see that well," Jean says of her father, who greeted visitors at the combination family reunion/birthday celebration with vocal welcomes and firm handshakes. He also proudly showed off two framed birthday notes: one from the White House signed by President George W. Bush and First Lady Laura Bush, another from U.S. Rep. Peter DeFazio.

Jerry has farmed in Malin for decades but also served eight years as a county commissioner from 1951 to 1959. Don Rajnus, Jerry's nephew, says his uncle's term was marked with two notable happenings: a shooting that nearly took his life and the fulfillment of a campaign promise to pave country roads outside of Klamath Falls. "None of the roads out here were paved," Don says. "He promised to have them paved and by the time he ran for a second term, they were."

The shooting happened in January 1957. Guy E. Cramer, a welfare recipient who was unhappy with the size of his monthly check, entered a meeting of the welfare board with two hidden weapons. Cramer shot commissioner Fred Peterson and administrator Altha Earkhard before shooting Jerry in the back. Earkhard was injured. Peterson was killed instantly and so, it was thought, was Jerry, who was pronounced dead. At the hospital, however, the doctor injected Jerry with a new serum and, as Jerry writes in "My First 100 Years," his newly published personal history, "about an hour later, I was able to breathe and hear voices." Jerry has been vocal ever since.

© LEE JUILLERAT

PHOTOS COURTESY JERRY RAJNUS

CLOCKWISE FROM TOP: Jerry holds his book, "My First 100 Years." ▪ Working the Oliver tractor, late '30s. ▪ Jerry and Helen, shortly after they were married in 1932.

His hearing isn't so sharp, but Jerry is still an animated stand-up host. "I'm the commissioner who got shot in the courthouse. I'm still here," he says with evident pride. Granddaughter Tricia Cole adds, "We've been having big birthday celebrations every five years since he turned 65! After he was shot and in the hospital, we were worried that he might not live very long. We didn't think he'd outlive us all."

Tricia spent part of her life growing up with her grandfather and grandmother Helen, who died in 1986, and now lives in San Diego. "I considered him my dad," she says of Jerry, who is known as "Uncle Jerry" to most everyone in Malin. "He was my father figure. Grandpa taught me to ride a horse, and my grandmother taught me how to entertain. Grandpa was a farmer: potatoes, wheat, alfalfa, everything. He was strict and I was afraid of him."

Several family members, like Don and his son Gavin, are still potato farmers. "He helped get Malin on the map when it came to selling potatoes to the San Francisco Bay Area. Once the people down there had these Malin potatoes, they didn't want the Idaho potatoes," Don says, noting that Jerry also helped develop a potato-packing business in the San Francisco area.

"He was a farmer with a lot of other interests," Don says in tribute. "But he was a farmer first."—*Lee Juillerat*

CALIFORNIA . SPRING 1993

Claire O'Rourke, 108

Many pots on a woodstove.

It is 1992 and we are having breakfast, three days before Christmas, with Claire Cayot O'Rourke. She is a healthy 108 and the oldest known survivor of the 1906 San Francisco earthquake. She wears a bright red flowered dress and a red sweater, with a Christmas corsage from the seniors' luncheon the day before. Her gnarled fingers have discreetly polished nails. Her hair is curled. Younger relatives remember her mother as having dark hair well into her 80s, but think that Claire may be using "a little auburn rinse."

© LINDA DUFURRENA

ABOVE: Claire at 108, still helping seniors with their tax returns. RIGHT: The family of Claire Cayot O'Rourke. Top row, standing: Claire Josephine Cayot (known as "Tot"), Frank, Eva. Front row, seated: Theophile, "Baby" Joe, "Mother" Claire Quigley Cayot, Ramon, and Francis "Father" Cayot.

Claire was born in January 1885. Chester A. Arthur was president. There were no cars, just horses and horse-drawn buggies. There was no electricity, no telephone, no radio. Home was La Porte, California, a little town near the headwaters of the Feather River, high in the Sierra Nevada. Gold Country.

"I must have been twelve the first time I left home," Claire recalls. "I went to San Francisco with my father. The street lights were of gas. The men would come along and light the lights. Oh, to have lights at night! I thought they were beautiful."

Her parents owned the Union Hotel in La Porte. Francis Cayot was an Old World patriarch, 50 before he married Claire's mother, Clarie Hinda Quigley, who was just twenty. Known as the "snowshoe bride," she married in Grass Valley and hiked from the wedding site across the winter meadows to her new husband's wooden hotel.

PHOTO COURTESY CLAIRE O'ROURKE

The young Claire was the oldest of eight siblings. She helped with the laundry, sometimes 40 sheets a day in the summer. "The boys took care of the horses in the livery barn across the street," she says. "Father would come up from Marysville with the wagon loaded with groceries—barrels of corned beef and corned pork, eggs, flour. The boys would haul the barrels down to the basement and I would cook using those big heavy iron pots on a woodstove."

The woodstove is still her cooking appliance of choice. She prefers slow cooking, saying it brings out the flavor in meat. "Of course, you worked for it," she admits. "You have to fill the fires, and when you bake you have to know just how much wood and how hot." Claire says there was always meat, usually three times a day. "Ham or bacon for breakfast, some kind of roast or stew for lunch, and steaks at night."

Father Cayot had a bar out front in the hotel where he served the men drinks while his wife and children stayed in the back. "He lived his life out there; we lived ours in the back. Poppa was strict about everything. We never questioned anything, we just lived."

In 1905, at the age of twenty, Claire married neighbor Leonard O'Rourke. They moved to San Francisco. It would be more exciting than their little mountain village. The following year a baby was well on the way when the great earthquake rocked the city. With thousands of others, Len and Claire camped in the tent city that grew in Golden Gate Park. Claire's only son, named Francis after her father, greeted a world of chaos. With $50 earthquake assistance from the city of San Francisco, the O'Rourkes moved back to the gold country.

Len pioneered downhill ski racing in the Sierra and helped organize groups of young people from his area in contests with neighboring villages. "They had tremendous skis, twenty feet long," Claire says. "The dope they put on them to make them slide was a big secret."

Len carried the mail, had other small businesses, and skied through the winters. "Francis and Len had snowshoe races when we lived up at Mohawk," Claire recalls fondly. She was happy; their marriage was a good one.

In 1931, Len became Plumas County supervisor; sixteen years later, he was elected county treasurer. The little family moved "down the hill" into the white frame house in Quincy, the county seat. Claire still lives in that same house. "It's comfortable," she says, "and I'm not afraid to live alone."

Len served just two years as treasurer before he died, and Claire was appointed to finish his term. She ran successfully for four more terms and in her last term, she also served as the county tax collector. She "retired" at age 78. But a museum employee from the local historical society says that Claire just refocused her energy on the Quincy Senior Citizens' Nutrition Program, and in 1963 became that organization's treasurer. She still helps seniors with their Social Security and their taxes, "and she still counts the lunch money."

Claire's biscuits and gravy are nearly finished. She will take the last sausage home for a snack later. "When you stop to look back, you just wonder how you did those things," she says with a grin, "but you just naturally did 'em. Crazy. I was fourteen going on fifteen when the 1800s ended and the 1900s began. I would sure like to see the year 2000."

—*Carolyn Dufurrena*

NEBRASKA . FALL 1997

George Younkin, 87

Bucking out broncs.

When George came to the Nebraska Sandhills in 1920, fresh from a Lincoln orphanage, the country was full of cow horses. "You'd point a cow out to them," he remembers, "and they could take her out of the herd or whatever you wanted to do."

Mr. and Mrs. Younkin were getting on in years and, with the children grown and gone, needed someone to help around the ranch. Quite a challenge for a sickly ten-year-old Hispanic youngster who had never been on a horse. George didn't know a saddle from a bridle, but says it doesn't take long to learn when someone is making fun of you. During a year of hospital confinement just prior to arriving in the Sandhills, he had plenty of time to dream. "I always thought of coming where I could be a cowboy. There were only one or two cars in Mullen when I got off that train," he says. "Most everyone was in wagons or on horseback, and that suited me."

In 1920, at ten years old, George was adopted and taken to the Nebraska Sandhills. He married Rana. "It must have been okay. We had eight kids."

PHOTOS COURTESY GEORGE YOUNKIN

George remembers helping deliver a trainload of Texas steers that came into Whitman the year he was eleven. Cowboys spent about a week in town awaiting the shipment, passing time in saloons or bucking out a few broncs down Main Street. "I thought I was as big as any of 'em," he chuckles.

"Wages were a dollar a day and we sometimes worked eighteen hours," he recalls. "But I liked it. I always liked working where there was a crowd, like on the Carver, and Big Creek. I never had any trouble getting a job."

The young cowboy began his own herd by buying cull cows from some of his employers and putting them out on shares. "One time the foreman of the Carver offered to trade me his 1932 Chevrolet for my cows," he laughs. "I should have done it. I lost half my herd that winter."

George met his wife on one of the big outfits. "Rana's mother was the cook. I got to taking Rana to dances and finally asked her to marry me. She thought it would be all right, and I guess it was. We had eight kids," he grins. "With 23 grandchildren and several great-grandkids, we're pretty well represented!"

In 1948, the Younkins bought part of the HL Bar where he has ranched ever since. After Rana's death, George sold the house, but he hasn't retired. "I still ride when my son Clyde lets me."

George has been in two serious horse wrecks since his 80th birthday, first breaking his pelvis, then a shoulder. Both times he claims to have been at fault rather than the horse. "Those doctors told me I healed quicker than most younger guys," he says, with more than a hint of pride.

"I've worked hard, but I've had a lot of fun in my life," George adds. "Right up the valley is the old home place where we lived for quite a few years. It's pretty well fallen down now. Never was much, but you know, my Rana never once complained."—*Lyn DeNaeyer*

From the beginning, they called Nevada a lonely place, even a wasteland. Yet many in search of silver mountain treasure discovered surprising beauty and mystery in the miles of rich hidden valleys they found like secrets in the shadows.

BACK SIDE OF WINNEMUCCA MOUNTAIN, NORTHERN NEVADA. PHOTO © LINDA DUFURRENA

Jack Rice, 83

Couldn't stay out of trouble.

A blue-eyed Irish pugilist, his ranching life behind him, his sheep, cattle and horses sold and his war years as commander of an LST (Landing Ship, Tank) in the South Pacific long past, Jack Rice continues in the world of agriculture as a brand inspector based in Elko County, Nevada. His beloved border collie, Jennifer, goes everywhere with him and, on this day, shares beef ribs for lunch.

Jack was born December 14, 1919, in San Francisco but was sent, as a grade-school lad, to Los Gatos, California, to his father's friend, because "I couldn't stay out of trouble," he says. "Fighting all the time." He started riding horses in Los Gatos and finished high school there. Then he went to Stanford University in Palo Alto, where he majored in political science. "After I graduated, work was scarce, so I took a job at the South San Francisco Union Stockyards."

Jack "really liked livestock," so he enrolled at the University of California at Davis to study animal science. He graduated with a master's in 1941 "and then, because all of us young men knew we were going to war, I signed up." He was sent to midshipman school in Chicago and became a 90-day-wonder. "The first time I heard thunder back there in Illinois, I thought we were being bombed," he says, laughing. "I'd never before been east of the Mississippi."

Not big, but mighty, Jack boxed for Stanford for four years and continued for another four in the Navy. "To tell the truth, I was a damn good boxer," he says in his husky voice, "but I paid for it. I've had cataracts removed from both eyes, got cauliflower ears and probably that's why I need to wear hearing aids."

As commander of an LST, Jack spent 1942 to 1946 in the Marshall and Gilbert islands, Taipan, Okinawa, and the Philippines. He was discharged as lieutenant commander. He married Kitty in 1943.

Jack's career in the livestock industry included working as a dairy field man and running his own Rice Livestock Company in Alturas from 1954 to 1984. He ran 850 mother cows, grew hay and had sheep, as many as 5,000 at one time.

Meanwhile, he sired three good

"I was a damn good boxer, but I paid for it. I've had cataracts, cauliflower ears, and I need to wear hearing aids."

CLOCKWISE FROM TOP LEFT: Jack with his dog, Jennifer. ▪ Commander Rice aboard his LST in World War II. ▪ Jack castrates a lamb in Gerlach, Nevada. ▪ Taking a break at Rice Livestock in Alturas, California, in 1955 with Barbara Chrysler (center) and Mrs. Bud Driscoll. ▪ Jack holds his daughter Sally in the 1940s.

PHOTOS COURTESY JACK RICE

kids: Mike, now a logger in Oregon and California; Sally, a teacher in California; and Tom, who lives in Nevada.

When he moved to Nevada, Jack came with his second wife Ricky (Stephens) and 3,000 ewes to Elias Goicoechea's range on the Holland Ranch on June 4, 1979. "We had the sheep at Goicoechea's Beaver Creek Division near North Fork and Mountain City and walked them from Beaver Creek to Eureka to pasture from Copper Basin to Duckwater. It took 23 days to make the trip every year."

The sheep were sold in 1985. He was paying 21.5 percent interest to the bank, the coyotes were taking twenty percent of the lamb crop and he had four herders to pay. "There was nothing left for me."

He still despairs about losing his beloved ranch in Alturas. "You want to hear about the Big Wreck?" He had borrowed from Wells Fargo Bank in 1977 and then "stupid as hell" went to Production Credit Association. "They told me I had to have more than the 850 head of cattle I had or they wouldn't loan me money. I knew better, but I needed the loan, so I bought another 750 and the next spring I couldn't give the calves away."

The bottom dropped out of the cattle business in the late '70s. "I put the calves in a feedlot in Surprise Valley and the PCA gave my note to Farmers Home Administration. I lost it all. Paid half a million back to the FHA."

When he bought that ranch, his best friend, Wilbur Huntington, was on it and he was still on it when Jack sold it. "In the 30 years we worked together, we never had a cross word. I miss Wilbur as much as I miss the ranch and I miss Alturas something fierce." However, as a brand inspector, Jack gets to see the country and to be around livestock. He's been inspecting since 1985 and, at 83, has no plans to quit.

He says he's enjoyed his life. "I don't think I'd change an awful lot." His parting words are, "Thanks, Wilbur."

—Mary Branscomb

OREGON . SPRING 2009

Mary Lois DeCourcey, 91

Taking a deep seat.

Mary Lois Savage was born in August of 1917 and raised by her Uncle Ray Adams on a 5,000-acre wheat ranch in the Palouse country near Colfax, Washington. There was nothing easy about the life, but it built good character. There were always chores to do: chickens to feed, eggs to gather, a garden to tend, produce to put up in the root cellar, laundry to do, and meals to cook on the woodstove.

"The real fun started at harvest time with the horse-drawn combines when the threshing crews needed to be fed so time was at a premium and days were long."

ABOVE: Chore time for Mary Lois included feeding the chickens. LEFT: Mary Lois with Mama Florence and Uncle Ray Adams in 1919.

PHOTOS COURTESY MARY LOIS DECOURCEY

Mary Lois learned to ride her cousin Lucille's pony but had no horse of her own until her tenth birthday, when Uncle Ray presented her with a saddle and shortly thereafter with an ex-cutting horse from the Pendleton Roundup named Midget. "At just over fourteen hands and near twenty years old, Midget was deemed too small and too old to continue her career in the rodeo." Riding time was limited because of the never-ending chores but her fondest memories are of riding Midget over the long rolling hills off the Palouse, chasing sunrises and sunsets and all that's between.

In 1934, after she left for school at the University of Idaho, Uncle Ray sold Midget and life moved on as she earned her degree in Latin with an English minor, Phi Beta Kappa. It was also at college that she met her future husband Jim DeCourcey, who hailed from Jacques Spur, Idaho. They wed in 1941. A career teaching Latin and English and raising her three children in southern Oregon, and the last twenty years after Jim's passing, traveling the world with friends and family, kept the thoughts of riding buried deeply, but never forgotten.

Last spring, at 90, she and her son Jim took a trip to Mexico. Part of their adventure was a ride with dudes. Turns out she was the most experienced rider in the group. So she made the trip as assistant wrangler and led, while the head wrangler worked up and down the line keeping the true neophytes in hand.

"Nothing amazed me more than this," Mary Lois says, "that I could ride for three hours and not get sore after 70 years away from horse and saddle."

Those hours in the saddle melted all the years. "I was neither stiff nor sore from the effort. It seems taking a deep seat never leaves the heart, soul or backside."

—David R. DeCourcey

Tom Irwin Jr., 91

The huge explosion barely missed the house.

Tom Irwin Jr.'s life reads like the best a country can offer. And though at the age of 91 he says emphysema and a "faulty heart" have slowed him down, his voice still carries the passion of a life lived with conviction—in his work as an engineer, but perhaps more sincerely, his life as a rancher.

Tom was born in Grand Rapids, Michigan, in 1906, one of three children. His mother was a singer who tried out for the Metropolitan Opera. She came home to nurse a sore throat, met Tom Irwin, and never returned. Tom Junior's father was a surgeon, who eventually became a professor of medicine at Grand Rapids Medical College.

Tom's parents owned 40 acres on the shore of Lake Michigan and summers during his youth were spent on that land. "I had my Jersey cow, one sheep, a chicken and a saddle horse," he says. "That was my introduction to agriculture." It was an introduction he would return to full time—not in his native Michigan, but in the northwest.

Tom and family moved to California in the 1930s for his job as manager of the West Coast office of Jenkins Brothers Valve Corporation. While there, he belonged to a club that had a polo field, racetrack, and a show ring. "I had a saddle horse there, and we had a riding club and trail right down through the Schilling estate. It was a beautiful thing. My wife and I liked the country. I decided we would find some sort of farm or ranch to satisfy the boys."

In 1961, he quit his job and moved with his three sons to Cheshire, Oregon, and a new life with his old love, agriculture. In the beginning, the farm was 100 acres, with lots of timber and a river running through it. To use the floor of the valley, Tom figures they pulled 250 stumps. He laughs and says, "We had a whole year of timber to burn!"

A memorable incident was when his son mixed explosives in a coffee can to blow up some of the stumps. "When it blew, it sent a huge explosion," Tom says, chuckling. "It missed the house by three feet." The family recovered 30 acres by eliminating the stumps. They also built a dam, installed an irrigation system, and brought in a small flock of sheep to help their main crop—lawn seed.

"You know why we bought sheep?" Tom will patiently ask. "Why, they help the root system to spread by pushing the seeds into the ground. Sheep are very important if you are going to raise crops of seeds." Over time, in addition to successful seed farming, the Irwins joined the California Sheep Growers Association and attended high-priced sheep shows with their Suffolks.

Tom moved back to Grand Rapids in 1991. Age and a sore back from his years of working with sheep finally got the best of him, but he misses his Oregon ranch. Today, from his Michigan apartment vantage post, he talks about the tremendous strains on farming, ranching and raising sheep that make it a tough business.

His son, Tom Irwin III, became an officer in the Suffolk Sheep Society and showed their prize ovines. "The shows took us back to the Midwest markets and it was beginning to appear that U.S. sheep were finally finding a place in the sun. Then came the Sierra Club, the spotted owl, changes in permits for grazing on public land, increased pasture prices, changes too numerous to mention. Our markets started falling away, the packing plant closed, the big flocks in the south started selling out. Oregon is particularly hit since whole towns are closing as the lumber mills go out of business."

PHOTOS COURTESY TOM IRWIN

CLOCKWISE FROM TOP: Tom displays sheep showmanship. ▪ Tom, age four, astride an early Reo car fitted out for a Grand Rapids parade. He is flanked by his mother and uncle. ▪ Tom Irwin Jr. is surrounded by his three sons, from left, Patrick, Toby and Tom III.

Still, two of his sons continue to work the Oregon farm, but it's tough. "The taxes are so severe now, you have to use land right up to the fence," Tom says. "It's awful hard to find pastureland."

Farms are also feeling the pinch from developers who, according to Tom, are "taking over, building big malls" where open land once was. "The parking lots [alone]," he says, "would make someone a good farm!"—*Patt Quinn-Davis*

Buck Clements, 85

No vegetarian.

A person's background has a lot to do with his future. Buried deep in Buck Clements' cedar chest is a rich legacy. Born in the tiny rural community of Corum, Oklahoma, Buck learned the meaning of hard work at the feet of his father and grandfather. He also learned what it was like to be a Native American living in a white man's world. Buck's grandfather was full-blooded Comanche. "Grandad didn't want to be listed as a tribe member," Buck says. "He was proud of his heritage, but he didn't want to be given anything. He wanted to work for a living on his own farm and ranch."

As a teenager working on a Works Progress Administration crew, Buck experienced racial discrimination firsthand when he was denied service at a local cafe. "My survey crew wanted beer with their lunch, but the cafe owner said he couldn't serve beer to Indians," Buck says. "I didn't like it, but I understood it was the law."

At $2.40 a day, the survey work was good pay, but the education was even better. Buck learned everything he could about soil conservation and livestock. He was determined to make a career in agriculture.

Blessed with athleticism and a muscular body, the six-foot, 185-pound country boy was awarded a football scholarship at nearby Cameron University. But before the first snap of the football, Buck was recruited to join the livestock judging team. "I knew more about livestock than football," Buck says, "and the [judging team] coach said it would help my future."

After transferring to Oklahoma A&M (now Oklahoma State University), Buck earned a Bachelor of Science degree in soil science and agronomy. Although accurate records were not kept on such things, Buck believes he may have been the first Native American to graduate from OSU's College of Agriculture.

"My survey crew wanted beer with their lunch, but the cafe owner said he couldn't serve beer to Indians."

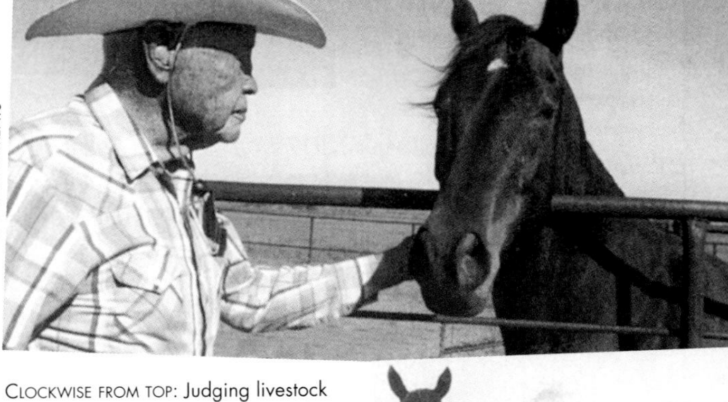

PHOTOS COURTESY BUCK CLEMENTS

CLOCKWISE FROM TOP: Judging livestock earned Buck the trophy as Outstanding Ag Freshman at Cameron University, Lawton, Oklahoma. ▪ Buck and Irene today. ▪ Buck's favorite horse is Princess, a quarter horse mare. ▪ While working for the feds to protect the prairie, Buck found time for his ranch and family.

For the next 35 years, he worked as a soil scientist and conservationist for the U.S.D.A. Soil Conservation Service in several Oklahoma locations. During this time he developed a compassion for working with people and protecting natural resources. When he wasn't mapping out a conservation plan for landowners to protect the fragile Oklahoma prairie, Buck was in the saddle working the family farm and ranch in southern Oklahoma.

The only interruption to his routine was World War II. Recruited by the Navy, Buck used his mechanical skills to repair aircraft engines. Returning home to his young wife, Irene, he settled into a healthy, active life that produced three children, a ton of patience and the yearning to farm. "All along we knew we wanted to return to the family farm," Buck says. "We just didn't know when." Retirement from the Soil Conservation Service in 1975 gave him time to expand the farm and move the homestead to "a good piece of ground."

Years of hard work beneath the hot Oklahoma sun have slowed Buck, but he continues to find time and energy to occasionally "horse" the tractor around the field. "I start every day with something to look forward to," Buck says. "Working in the field, helping the neighbors, just something to help our community."

Buck's desire to help others, combined with good genes and a healthy diet peppered with ample doses of red meat are the main reasons the sturdy Oklahoman gives for his longevity.

"None of that vegetarian stuff for me," Buck says. "Just give me some good beef!"

—*Sam Knipp*

Aury Smith, 84

The whirling-dancing ride.

Evening's shadows are dimming the Surprise Valley sky as Aury Smith totes cardboard boxes stuffed with provisions for the week ahead. The containers are filled with delights like leftover raspberry pie and, jammed inside a recycled Quaker Oats container, stacks of homemade chocolate chip cookies. There are also necessities—towels, eggs and lantern fuel—all carefully packed by Aury's wife, Violet.

During milder seasons Violet, 69, sets herself in the pickup alongside her 84-year-old husband. But during the winter she mostly stays behind at their Cedarville, California, home, content to join him on weekends or wait for the nights he returns to town. Like new lovers they hold hands, lightly touching each other. And before Aury leaves for the 24-mile, 45-minute drive over the Hays Range to their isolated Nevada ranch, Violet opens his door and passes over a last carton of supplies. She and Aury hug and kiss, and trade whispered words of affection.

Aury's enjoying life, but he also remembers World War II—the nightly bombings in and near London, driving heavy equipment off landing barges to the shores of Normandy Beach two days after D-day, ferocious counterattacks by German soldiers, and the depression that set in during the terrors of the Battle of the Bulge, the last, unsuccessful effort by the Germans to push back invading Allied troops. "I didn't know if I'd come back from that or not," admits Aury.

Aury prefers small towns and, even better, lonely ranches. "You don't have to put up with the traffic, with barking dogs, and you don't have kids with those darn boom boxes."

Aury comes by his solitude naturally. He was born March 26, 1916, in Ioha, Utah, a community so small that it has disappeared from maps. "Dad used to trade horses. He'd track horses for two or three days and come back with a bunch," Aury says with obvious pride. "I think our life was pretty rough there—I went to bed hungry a lot of nights."

The family set out for California in 1924 but was waylaid in Idaho, where his father, William "Bill" Smith, and family found work harvesting beets. Aury was only a boy. "It didn't hurt me. Done me good."

The Smiths—father, mother Maude, six sisters and two brothers—left Idaho in April 1928. Traveling in two covered and two open wagons, they were heading for Redding, California. It was early July when they passed through Surprise Valley and camped for the night on Cedar Pass. Some valley ranchers offered them work harvesting hay and they never left.

PHOTOS COURTESY AURY SMITH

CLOCKWISE FROM TOP: A wild ride in Alturas, 1940. ▪ Aury and colt, ca. 1929. ▪ Violet gives Aury a kiss as he leaves for the ranch. ▪ Aury and Orrin sport camel-hide chaps in New Pine Creek, Oregon.

© LEE JUILLERAT

As a teenager, Aury handled a six-horse team, "working here and there, wherever I could get a job." He left school after the eighth grade. "I was just a kid and some of those buckaroos were 75 years old. They taught me a lot."

Aury took to horses and ranch work naturally. He rode saddle and bareback broncs in rodeos all over the West, including the 1939 San Francisco World's Fair. He loved the whirling-dancing ride. "Just in your world by yourself when you're there," explains Aury, his eyes twinkling, describing the emotions he experienced while trying to stay atop a jackknifing bronc. "I liked every mean, dang horse I could get."

He saved enough money from his winnings and jobs to buy a ranch west of Alturas. But with the war approaching, he turned the ranch over to his brother, Orrin. Drafted into the Army in 1942, Aury was sent to Fort Riley, Kansas, to work with the horse cavalry but soon transferred to an engineering division as a heavy equipment operator. He spent 23 months in England building airstrips—and dodging bombs. He remembers the near nightly raids.

"The Germans would wait 'til you got in bed and got warm and they'd send the planes over and you'd have to go into foxholes." Aury feared for his life but, as had happened in England, Normandy and on the march through France, he survived. He was on his way to Italy when the Germans surrendered so he returned to France. When others learned of his horseback skills, Aury was asked to help organize a rodeo for Allied troops. When more than 50,000 soldiers wanted to attend the first rodeo in a makeshift ball field with seating for 5,000, plans were quickly made for more rodeos. Aury and other military cowboys shuttled around Germany over the next three months arranging and staging rodeos. He rode bulls and saddle broncs "and had several winnings."

They gathered horses from everywhere, sometimes trading crates of oranges and cartons of cigarettes for stock. "If they'd buck good, we'd either back off or jump off so as not to discourage them. We just put on shows and had lots of fun." After his discharge, he and brother Reed signed on to feed 1,500 head of cattle at the legendary MC Ranch in Adel. "They had a cook house and fed good."

Aury met Violet on a blind date in New Pine Creek. They were married June 27, 1948, and had three children. He leased the Cold Springs Ranch in 1950 and bought it in 1960. The ranch is 24 miles from Cedarville, near Vya, a remote highway maintenance station. Aury ran a small cow-calf operation and raised high-protein, dairy-quality alfalfa.

In 1956 he began working for the Vya highway station, a job he held for 32 years. Before and after work he did ranch chores.

Aury has kept 160 acres, including a fish pond, outbuildings, corrals and the old Kimball homestead cabin that's been remodeled and expanded to a comfortable, no-frills three-bedroom ranch house heated by a woodstove and lit by gas lights and lanterns. Heat from the stove warms the hot water tank.

"I do my housework about two days before wife moves back," he grins. Outside, the desert air is rich with the heady aroma of sagebrush. "I could exist in town," smiles Aury, "but I wouldn't be living."—*Lee Juillerat*

MONTANA . SPRING 2006

Susan Haughian

Irish red-headed legend.

A century ago Susan Haughian stepped off a train on a hot October afternoon in the roaring, rustic cowtown of Miles City, Montana, and saw nothing but brown, dusty landscape in all directions. As the youngest child of a successful Irish businessman, Susan had been served by maids, and had watched as her older sisters did all the cooking and sewing. She was used to a large, comfortable house surrounded by a cool, damp, green world.

"Her first words in the new land were, 'Good Lord! What have I done?'" says granddaughter Patty Neiffer.

When Dan Haughian returned to Ireland to marry his fiancée, he discovered that she hadn't waited, so he married her younger sister, Susan, pictured here in Ireland, October 5, 1905. BELOW: Susan and her five daughters, from left: Susan, Kathleen, Dorothy, Helen and Tessie. The small girl is probably a granddaughter. Susan and Dan also had five sons.

"Her early experiences in cooking were hilarious," Patty continues. "She borrowed a cookbook, and was totally puzzled by instructions. When she saw the cake recipe calling for icing she almost panicked. 'Heaven help me. In this country you need ice to make a cake!'"

During those early days she served things that the men put in their pockets and later buried outdoors, but over the years she learned to cook and bake for a growing family and a large work crew.

Her husband Dan worked hard and bought every piece of land he could afford. Many homesteaders walked away from their claims—and Susan bought them for next to nothing.

Dan gave Susan two very important things before he died suddenly in 1931 at the height of the Great Depression. He gave her ten children (five boys and five girls) and he gave her orders: "Never sell your land," he said. "Fight for it. Without land you're just a drifter."

Her children report that for almost a year after Dan's death, Susan stayed in her room and cried. She refused to talk to anyone. But when she finally came out she was ready to take on the world. She had decided to become the biggest and best rancher in Montana.

When others were folding and fleeing during tough times, Susan bought abandoned ranches far and wide, filling them with Haughian men and their workers.

When asked why she had never remarried, she laughed and demanded, "What man in his right mind would marry a woman with ten kids?"

At the time of her death in 1972 she was worth millions as the owner of one of Montana's most successful ranches, with thousands of cattle and sheep roaming over 240,000 acres.

—*Bill Kiley*

PHOTOS COURTESY HAUGHIAN FAMILY

Dogs in Texas, like country dogs everywhere, love the road. They're the near-enough official first greeter for anybody coming to visit and the always reliable welcome-home party for the ones they're glad to see. In some places, roads still haven't become too important to exclude good dogs.

DOGS ON THE ROADWAY, ROUTE 66. PHOTO © LARRY ANGIER

WEST
LOOP
271
OLD
ROUTE
66
NORTH
291
WEST
LOOP
271

Hallie Stillwell, 98

Trust everyone, but brand your cattle.

"I've been staring at the same countryside for years and it looks different every time. There's still a lot to look at, so I don't have time to feel old," says 98-year-old Hallie Stillwell of Brewster County, Texas. Miss Hallie, as her friends call her, is loaded down with her old 12-gauge shotgun, posing for photos. She quips, "I feel like Annie Oakley."

She was born in Waco, Texas, on October 20, 1897. Nine years later, her papa, Guy Crawford, quit his job at Fulton Meat Market "and packed his people in two Conestoga wagons and headed northwest for New Mexico." Three years later, they moved back to Texas along with many other heartbroken settlers. By then, Hallie was twelve and could handle a wagon herself.

After graduation from Normal School in Marfa in 1916, Hallie began teaching in Presidio, Texas, across the Rio Grande from Pancho Villa's revolution. She was ready to go, but Papa warned that she would be going on a wild goose chase. Her reply was, "then I'll go gather my geese."

In 1918, Hallie met and married local cowboy Roy Stillwell. His ranch hands were not thrilled when Roy brought home "that schoolteacher" to their one-room ranch house. She was a real problem and couldn't be left alone because of the bandito trouble, and they couldn't take her with them because her skirts spooked the horses.

When they felt it safe to leave her at home, she cleaned the coffee pot so that it wouldn't make good coffee for six months. The same day, she washed the writing off all the woodwork, except the words on the door, *"Help yourself to the food, wash the dishes, and put the cat out."* Years of ranch records were destroyed. Hallie only left the ranch to go to Marathon to give birth to her three children: Roy (called Son), Dadie and Guy. There were no anesthetics and she says, "It was without a sniff of anything."

In the 1930s, many people realized the significance of the canyons where Hallie lived. She started arm-twisting and by the mid-1940s, Big Bend National Park became a reality.

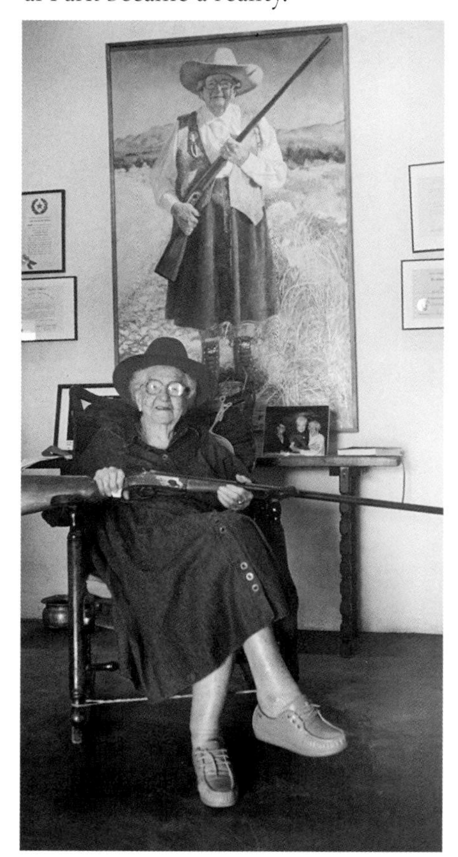

PHOTOS COURTESY STILLWELL FAMILY

CLOCKWISE FROM LEFT: Current portrait of Hallie with 12-gauge shotgun. The background painting is by Alix Camille Dunn of Houston.
- Rubye Richardson (Burcham) and Hallie (right) wear customary full-length riding outfits, ca. 1914.
- Roy Stillwell, ca. 1914.
- Hallie's 1916 graduation photo.

Tragedy struck shortly after, in 1948. Roy was killed while driving a hay truck when it overturned at a curve in the road. Hallie was devastated but still had the ranch, and the banker told her, "I'll help you feed your cattle but not help feed your family." There was a market for wax, so she started harvesting the ranch's candelilla plants for the wax that they produced, with the help of a Mexican crew. She boiled the plants in large vats of water and sulfuric acid. The wax was skimmed off the top and put into barrels for transport and sale. The income kept the family fed.

In 1956, she began working as a journalist and hotel manager. Eight years later, Hallie became Justice of the Peace for Precinct 1 of Brewster County. This meant new duties, from weddings to trying misdemeanor cases and serving as coroner.

Miss Hallie's present career began in 1979, operating the Stillwell Store and R.V. Park located south of Marathon. In 1991, with help from friends and family, her Hallie Stillwell Hall of Fame Museum was dedicated on her 94th birthday. It's the crowning glory for the woman who was the perennially reigning Chili Queen; the holder of the Stillwell "4L" brand registered in 1835 (a year before independence); the woman who sells a T-shirt in her store that says, "Trust everyone, but brand your cattle"; the woman who tucked a .38 Colt in her skirt when she was teaching at Presidio; and for the woman the governor of Texas certified, "Know ye, that Hallie Stillwell is hereby commissioned Yellow Rose of Texas."

—*Carolyn Fox*

Wiss & Mike Toomer, 83 & 80

Shadowing the stock.

One summer jingling horses, hauling water, and doing chores on a ranch in Burns, Colorado, convinced Livingston "Wiss" Toomer that he wanted to spend his life as a cowboy. For nearly 40 years the soft-spoken Virginian and his wife Mildred, a.k.a. "Mike," summered in cow camps. "Our lives shadowed the cattle," Mike says. "Up the mountain in summer and down for the winter."

"One day Mike found a pack rat in the baby's drawer, so she compelled me to hang the bassinet from the ceiling."

Wiss' first trip to Burns in the summer of 1941 was enough to scare off a meeker soul. The green eighteen-year-old caught a ride from Denver in a ranch pickup. The driver fell out of the truck on the Trough Road between Kremmling and State Bridge, swerving off the road in the process. Wiss stopped the pickup before things got really out of hand, and they managed to get back on the road and to the ranch without further incident.

Wiss fell in love with the cowboy life. After a winter trying to trap near Browning, Montana, he returned to Burns in the spring and took up residence in the Castle Creek cow camp. After shipping the cattle that fall of 1942, Wiss entered the U.S. Marine Corps. He saw action on Saipan and Iwo Jima, and was wounded three times. On his return, he attended Colorado A&M, earning a degree in animal science in 1949. About that time, his brother was dating a schoolteacher named Mildred Shiflett, also from Virginia. Wiss usurped his brother and married Mike in June 1951.

In the spring of '54, Wiss decided to return to Colorado and landed his old job in the Castle Creek camp. He introduced Mike to the life that he loved. Or, in her words: "We went from civilization to isolation." The altitude left her "asleep in camp" much of the first summer. She also had to teach herself to cook on the finicky woodstove. Her efforts—especially the desserts—soon became a hit among the cowboys. Despite cattle occasionally trampling the spring, and the stovepipe serving as a lightning rod in violent thunderstorms, she was willing to return the next summer.

By spring there was a baby to go along, too. "One day Mike found a pack rat in the baby's drawer," Wiss says, "so she compelled me to hang the bassinet from the ceiling."

Midnight feedings became a greater chore—after the stove was lit and a bottle made and heated, one of them had to balance on a chair to feed the baby. Even that didn't put Wiss and Mike off—the next year they packed two babies to camp. There were three sons in all, which was fortunate, according to Wiss: "I just wouldn't have known what to do with girls."

Wiss rose to be cow foreman, a job he held for fifteen years. He eventually leased the ranch on his own, but most enjoyed the summer camp life. His philosophy: "Put the cows where they don't want to be."

In 1966 he began a 36-year career as a special brand inspector for Colorado. "I saw quite a few changes on the range," Wiss says. "When I first came to Burns, the ranch ran about 3,000 steers. Forty-five years later, when I was leasing, the same place ran about 200 to 300 pairs."

In 1993 the ranch was sold by the Benton family who had employed Wiss for two generations. The Toomers moved to town. They're still getting used to it.

Wiss and Mike recall their camp days fondly. "If you call ten varieties of mice fond," says Mike. Five weeks removed from having both knees replaced simultaneously and already back on his feet, Wiss still longs for the rugged life. "All this modern stuff, all that's any good is the modern medicine and indoor plumbing."—*Tim Fitzgerald*

CLOCKWISE FROM TOP: Wiss and Mike with sons, left to right: Jim, Bob and Tom.
- Wiss still prefers the rugged life and taught his kids early about horses and cattle.
- Taking hay to the stock in a Colorado winter.
- Mike and Wiss on their wedding day in Virginia, 1951.

Vera Wagner, 82

Eating jackrabbits and dandelions.

Few people know more about Wagontire than Vera Addington Wagner. It is the Highway 395 wayside between Lakeview and Burns in eastern Oregon. It's a humble, population two, roadside cafe/gas station/motel that's mainly visited by travelers in need of a restroom, soft drink, hamburger or tank of gas. This is where Vera was born on July 7, 1918, on the family homestead a few miles from the present-day cafe. She was the youngest of Luther James and Loretta Addington's five children, one of two born in Wagontire.

Until she moved with her parents to Grants Pass, Oregon, in 1936, electricity and indoor plumbing were unknowns. The family lived on what began as a 160-acre homestead in 1913 and expanded as her father took over property abandoned by disillusioned settlers. "Those were the good old days. They were tough. We knew what hard work was."

The Addingtons came to Oregon from Dallas County, Iowa, because of her father's allergies. A doctor recommended a high, dry climate. The family settled in Bend until her father chose a homestead near Wagontire Mountain and moved in May 1913. "I've wondered about it for 82 years: Why did my dad ever settle where he did? Did he have to settle in an area without any water? That's what finally drove us out."

Water was always a problem. The Addingtons dug 32 wells, most of them shallow. "I was chipping with a pick and, bingo, we hit water," she remembers. "I yelled, 'Papa, we've got water.' I stood in the bucket and he winched me out." As the wells dried up in the summer, she gathered the milk cows and workhorses and walked them six miles to the nearest springs. "It's a different life out there."

Their main source of fuel was sagebrush, along with dried cow pies. Cows provided milk. The family "ate a lot of jackrabbits." In the spring, dandelions "made awfully good greens." Water was gathered by placing barrels under the eaves of their home and outbuildings. When temperatures dipped, filled barrels were allowed to freeze, stashed in haystacks, "and we'd have ice all winter."

In winter, cattle were butchered and hung on poles. Frozen beef was wrapped in canvas tarps and buried in the haystacks. "Our refrigerator was the middle of the haystack."

School was sporadic. "Teachers wouldn't stay," says Vera, recalling one who carried her suitcase to school and one day, after seeing dust on the roadway, bid her students adieu, flagged down the vehicle, and caught a ride.

Vera's mother, who served as postmistress from 1917 to 1931, changed the name of the post office from Egli, named for the original postmaster, to Wagontire, for the nearby mountain in 1919. "She wanted to change it as it seemed more fitting since we lived near Wagontire Mountain, also to have it put on the map." The name change, however, didn't happen until Vera's birth. "Mother sent in the application and was told the name could be changed but a town could not be mapped with a population under five," she explains. "My brother and sister were away from home, which left four in the family. So when I was born, Mother reen-

PHOTOS COURTESY VERA WAGNER

CLOCKWISE FROM TOP:
Luther James and Loretta Addington pose with their children: Melvin, Virgil, Vera, Lola and Lena in 1927. ■ Vera, age one. ■ Vera, Virgil, Carmen and Catherine play croquet in the desert, ca. 1929. ■ Sister Lola, seventeen, brother Virgil, nine, and Vera, six. CENTER: Vera today.

tered her application and it was accepted, putting Wagontire on the map."

Vera has other Wagontire memories. "The mail came once a week, except sometimes when the snow was too deep to get through. It came by horseback, buggy, bobsled and car. Mail day was a great day on the desert. People came from all over to get their mail, and nearly always stayed for dinner and sometimes even stayed overnight. One homesteader from Dry Valley, Ola Soderberg, had to come about 30 miles on horseback as there was no road to the valley. He would come every spring and again in the fall. He would get out our Montgomery Ward catalog, sit down and make an order for a whole new outfit. Warm clothes if it was in the fall and summer clothes in the spring."

He would stay overnight. "As he left in the morning he always said, 'See you in three weeks.' After three weeks had passed, here he was to get his new clothes. Oftentimes they would not be in the mail. If not, he would stay until the next week. Then he would open his package and say to Mother, 'Mrs. Addington, do you mind if I take a bath, I smelled of myself and I stink?' He would say this with a wide grin and a wink at us kids."

According to Vera, he would get out the big round bathtub and fill it with water from the reservoir on the side of the stove, run the kids out, put a chair under the doorknob and take a good bath. "After his bath, dressed in his new clothes from shoes to a new hat, Ola would drag the tub out on the porch, put it up on the wash benches, get some soap and the washboard and wash all his dirty ragged clothes in his bathwater and put them on the line to dry. Then he would roll them up, tie them on the back of his saddle, and head home. Many times we wouldn't see him again until it was time to order his next outfit of clothes."

Vera was eighteen when her family left Wagontire, "I cried all the way to Grants Pass." While there she met Louis Albert Wagner. They were married September 4, 1937, and had two sons. Louis died in 1990.

"There's nothing left of our place at all," grumbles Vera of her family ranch. "I loved it out there. I guess because it was my home. I miss it. I miss it a lot."—*Lee Juillerat*

CALIFORNIA . WINTER 2008

Louise Hanson, 92

Adjusting to nature.

PHOTOS COURTESY LOUISE HANSON

FROM TOP: Louise and friends with Kitty the mule and Dickie the pony, "an unlikely pair." ■ Louise with her cattle and horse, 2007.

At an age when most people are just trying to make it through the day, Louise Hanson is running the 14,000-acre Las Cruces Ranch in Santa Barbara County, California. Up before 5 a.m., she's had breakfast and fed the barn cats before she meets the hands to start the hard work at seven. "I feel so fortunate," she says, "to be able to be a part of our nation's food chain, and to be born in America. There is nothing I like more than to be out on the ranch among my cattle."

Born December 30, 1914, on the Moulton family's 21,000-acre El Toro Ranch, Louise learned to ride and rope at an early age. "As a child," she says, "I always felt so important when our foreman let me part out the fat steers for market or cull heifers for replacement. I was into everything—teams, saddle horses, cattle, farming."

When she was about five years old and her sister Charlotte was ten, her father bought them a beautiful sorrel pony, complete with wicker-seated pony cart from the parade entries at the historic Pasadena Tournament of Roses Parade. Louise named the sorrel Dickie, and he was with her for many years, even teaming with a gentle mule named Kitty to pull buggies.

Louise followed Charlotte to Pomona College, graduating in 1936. She then studied agriculture and business at Davis Ag College. "Then," she says, "before settling down to full-time ranching, I traveled to the Orient, Hawaii, Panama, New York, and Boston."

Why those particular places? "Because my sister went to Europe," she chuckles. "I wanted to go the other way."

Married three times ("I buried 'em all," she says.), Louise moved the family cattle from El Toro to the Las Cruces Ranch in 1972 with her third husband, Ivar Hanson. "For many years," she says, "I was buyer number one at the San Francisco Cow Palace bull sale. If I liked the Grand Champion, I bought him."

Although she lost her third husband to a tractor accident in 1979, Louise has remained committed to the Las Cruces Ranch. "This ranch is surrounded by the Santa Barbara and Santa Ynez mountain ranges," she says. "And with the Gaviota coastline, it gives us spectacular views. We can even see an occasional missile being fired from the nearby Vandenberg Air Force Base."

A back ailment finally forced Louise to stop riding, but she drives her truck to oversee all parts of the ranch operations. "You have to do different things," she says, "to adjust to what nature brings to you." The last year nature brought drought, but Louise has seen everything by now, and is not daunted.

"We farm some barley and we used to thrash it and sell the seed, but now we bale most of it for the cattle, or windrow it and leave it for the weaners or to fatten the steers for market. There's always, always plenty to do on the ranch, and that's what I wanta be doin'!"

—*Steve Thompson*

SHEEP AND GOATS ON THE HILL AT THE CUNEO RANCH NEAR CLINTON, CALIFORNIA. PHOTO © LARRY ANGIER

California was the promised land to many who would not be disappointed. Yet peaceful, gentle hillsides could not be claimed by all, and those who fenced them would need to defend them.

Dave Grove, 98

Keeping the outside thrown in.

The old boy's good looking, with fine silver hair and a wide smile. He was born on a ranch in 1894, and for most of his 98 years has worked around sheep and cattle.

Dave Grove's father worked for the XL Ranch, a southern Oregon desert outfit that ran about 20,000 cattle. But in the terrible winter of 1889-90, the weather claimed the lives of darn near everything. The family moved to Cedarville, California, then Eagleville to the south in Surprise Valley, and his father continued to work on ranches. But he also bought some sheep.

"I herded sheep 'til my eyes bugged out," Dave laughs. "My dad got hold of a bunch of sheep in 1910 and he took me out of high school and out in the Nevada desert. He set up a tent and me and my brother started herding those 1,200 sheep." The boys didn't know much about herding, but learned quickly by watching a Basque herder who had some sheep close by. "Hell," Dave says, "that Basco just turned them loose and kinda kept the outside thrown in and never bothered with them."

When his father sold the flock after two years, Dave went to work for Bill Scott and the S brand. He earned $30 a month and saved his money because he wanted to get into something for himself. "I never wanted to work for wages, and I'd look at the guys who had something and think, damn, if they can do it, I can."

There were dairies in Surprise Valley and there wasn't much demand for the offspring. He'd buy dairy calves because they were pretty cheap, and then he'd buy hay for them in wintertime. "In the summer, I'd turn them out on the range with the rest of the guys."

In 1917, he was called to the war in Europe, sold his (by now) 60 head of cattle, put his money in the bank, and went to France to fight. He was wounded on the front, came back to California in 1919, and married his sweetheart Ervine. He worked for another rancher, then leased a ranch, and finally bought a piece of his own near Eagleville. He ran cattle on the ranges of California and Nevada and he and Ervine had three sons.

They ran cattle on public land that looked different every year depending on moisture. "You read that ranchers devastated the land, and once people get that in their damn heads, you can't get it out. The first year I ran on the open range in the '30s it was wonderful. Grass grew up higher than the sagebrush all over the place. We had the moisture to do it. It was a good year. Other years you don't get it like that, so it doesn't look as good."

PHOTOS COURTESY DAVE GROVE

CLOCKWISE FROM TOP: The Grove homestead, called The Summer Kitchen, on the west side of Goose Lake, Oregon, ca. 1898. Dave is the little fellow on the left, surrounded by mother, brothers and sisters. ▪ Overton School, south of Cedarville, California. Dave is in the front row, third from left in striped shirt. His brother Ernest is next to him, fourth from left. ▪ Dave (left) and Ernest, a long time ago. ▪ At one time Dave, looking good at 98, ran 86 head of horses, including saddle horses and workhorses.

He used the 48 and 49 branding irons, and sold his grandsons 360 head of pregnancy-tested cows two years ago, "because," he chuckles, "I didn't want a problem if I died." But he still owns the ranch. Others in his family might have wanted a piece of it too, but he says, "You can only support so many people. Your cash flow won't take it, even on a good year."

Dave Grove doesn't help much with the cattle anymore. But almost every day you can find him working around the place, burning weeds in the irrigation ditches, fixing fences, clearing away the tules. He doesn't hear as well these days, but admits to turning up his hearing aid to hear the blackbirds or wild canaries in the enormous willows outside his house.

Ervine died 22 years ago and he's been "baching" it ever since. "It's pretty hard, when you have a wonderful woman like that, to ever be satisfied again. She gave me 52 years and we had a wonderful life."

The Grove Ranch runs east clear to Lower Lake in Surprise Valley. His land runs south a ways, north to the edge of a canyon. The main ranch buildings, including two houses (one built in 1870 and still in perfect shape), are fairly close together, but he refuses to change it. "I can't go spread out unless I cover up good meadow, and I don't want to do that."

It's been hard for Dave to retire because he has always been productive and hardworking. "I can't set around, I get nervous." He makes coffee or fixes lunch for visitors—even picking fresh watercress from his crick. He takes care of the home place, and often drives into Eagleville, Cedarville, or across the Black Rock Desert to the town where he used to winter sheep in the Truckee Meadows. That was around 1927 when Reno was a very small place.

If he catches his almost 99-year-old face in the mirror, he chuckles and says, "You old bastard, you are looking pretty rough." But his neighbors disagree. "That cowboy Dave Grove," one claims, "he's still dangerous in town!"

—*C.J. Hadley*

Secretarial school. Emily is front row, right.

CALIFORNIA . SUMMER 1999

Emily Matthews, 105

Born October 11, 1893, to German immigrants, Emily Schmeekle grew up in tiny Eustis, Nebraska, the seventh of twelve children. Room for misbehavior was slim to none. "I was really the first of a second group," she says. "My father had six grown children when he married my mother. She was twenty. He was 47." After Emily's mother died in childbirth, cooking chores fell to Emily. The German meals she prepared included hearty bacon and egg breakfasts, German breads and sausages, salads, ham, meat and potatoes. She says, "I didn't care much for fish."—*Roxyann Spanfelner*

CALIFORNIA . SUMMER 2005

Betty Bacchi, 82

Betty Jean Peterson was born in 1922 in Boulder, Colorado, the younger of two girls. Her father Clarence was a driller in the oil fields of Wyoming and Colorado. When she was a baby, the family lived in a tent. "It was so cold out there, the wind never quit blowing," Betty says. "The diapers would freeze before you could hang them up."—*Jacqueline Varozza*

CALIFORNIA . SUMMER 2001

John Edward Fischer, 103

Cattle growing goes back a long way in John's family. His grandfather, Andrew McQuade, and three brothers left Ireland for New York in the late 1840s. In 1961, the quartet made the arduous trip to California—not tempted by the glint of gold, but to fulfill their dreams of cattle ranching in the vast rangeland of the American West.

Cowboys ready to drive cattle from high country back to home ranch.

—*Patricia Ruthrauff*

NEVADA . FALL 2004

Lawrence Miller, 91

Born in Oregon in 1913, Lawrence quit school a week before his sixteenth birthday and took a job as a buckaroo. It was a nomadic life, moving from ranch to ranch with his two slick-fork saddles, bedroll and a couple of changes of clothes. "I was doing real good," Lawrence says. Most buckaroos in those days were doing real good if they owned one saddle.

His education and hard work paid off. In 1944, Bing Crosby bought the ranch Lawrence was managing and kept him on as ranch manager. While Lawrence would rather have been on a horse, he did enjoy taking care of the ranch, feeding the cattle and working with Crosby. "Bing was there a lot," he says. "He'd walk in, throw his hat in the corner, drink a cup of coffee and chat with the guys. Occasionally, he'd join them at the bar at Jack Creek. After a few drinks, he'd sing for the cowboys, and boy, could he whistle, too!"—*Sue Reynolds*

WASHINGTON . SUMMER 1994

Jerry Getz, 90

An old hand, still in the saddle.

By the time a cowboy reaches the age of 90, it's safe to assume he's yearning to get back in the saddle again. But not so for Jerry Getz because he's never paid much attention to his age, which is probably why he's still more at home in a saddle than in an easy chair.

The Tarboo Valley, near Quilcene on Washington's Olympic Peninsula, remains as it has been for decades. Like the valley in which he lives, Jerry clings to the lifestyle he has thrived in for nearly a century. This tenacity is the reason he was chosen the 1993 Old Hand. Since 1987, the Old Hand Committee in Haines, Oregon, has scoured the country annually for old cowhands still active in their craft. "I think it's quite an honor," says Jerry. "The knowledge that those old hands have is going to be lost one day."

Jerry's been horseback since he was a tiny kid. He drove horses at age four and was a full-fledged hand by six. He learned how to shoe horses in his dad's blacksmith shop. Little did he realize then that the skills learned at his father's knee would later serve him well.

His mother died when he was six, so Jerry worked for his room and board while trying to keep up with his studies. At nine, he was a water runner, and by age fourteen he was feeding 40 head of cattle. Not uncommon for that era, Jerry left school in the sixth grade. At fifteen, he was working on a ranch for $13 a month, plus room and board.

"If a guy was willing to work, he could get by," Jerry says. But he did more than just work. In the late 1930s, he also began what would become a twenty-year love affair with rodeos. His attempts to exhibit gutsy trick riding led him to organize small rodeos long before big-time rodeos were seen in western Washington.

In 1948, Jerry and his new wife Barbara moved to the 80-acre farm they still call home. Jerry says that adding the farm, "the perfect place to live," was the key to the good life he's shared with his wife and daughters, Linda and Patsy. "My best accomplishment in life," he says, "was getting this place."

For more than 40 years, Jerry traveled western Washington. He never called himself a farrier because he says it's just a fancy name for what he was—a horseshoer.

In the 1970s, Jerry—egged on by a friend's $10 bet he couldn't do it—did a vault and a croupier's jump off a horse's rear, all with a female trick rider also standing on the horse. He was 75 at the time.

In 1987, at 84, Jerry finally put away his horseshoeing tools, professionally at least. It took two knee-replacement surgeries to slow him down. "Cowboy knees," the doctor called them. Once Jerry mended, retirement became a relevant word. He's almost as active as ever, though, riding with Barbara and doing all the things necessary to take care of the farm.

"I've had a good life and I've worked hard," he says. "I have no regrets."—*Sandy Hershelman*

PHOTOS COURTESY JERRY GETZ

Jerry Getz began a decades-long love affair with rodeo in the late 1930s. His attempts to exhibit gutsy trick riding (shown here) led him to organize small rodeos long before big-time rodeos were seen in western Washington. LEFT: Jerry today. In 1993, he was chosen "Old Hand" by the folks of Haines, Oregon.

Geraldine Du Bois Perkins, 98

No time to sleep.

Turning 99 this year, Geraldine Perkins still has a wealth of spunk and a sense of humor. Legally blind since her twenties, Geraldine's other senses became sharper, giving her extra tenacity for life. With a grin she begins her life story: "I was born on a cold winter midnight, December 7, 1907, in Longton, Kansas, to Franklin and Mary Du Bois...."

Not long after her birth, her grandfather came to the small but thriving community of Corona, New Mexico, and opened a general store. The younger Du Bois family followed, left for a few years, then returned in 1916. Geraldine resumed her fifth-grade school year in the Corona school.

When she reached high-school age, her parents sent her by train to Silver City, New Mexico. They wanted her to graduate from an accredited high school, which was not available in Corona at the time. She graduated at the age of fifteen.

At the University of New Mexico she majored in biology and chemistry with her sights set on a career in medicine. But that was not to be. During a visit to her grandparents in Kansas, Geraldine realized something was wrong. She was diagnosed with retinitis pigmentosa, and her dreams of studying at Johns Hopkins ended with the reality that she was going blind.

"It just completely threw me," she says. "I gave up a teaching fellowship at the University of Nevada and came home. I took a job teaching at the little one-room school over the hill we called Punkin Center. I got paid $100 a month for nine months plus a $5-a-month janitor fee."

Geraldine followed her first year of teaching with another—teaching seventh and eighth grades in Tatum, New Mexico. "I like to say those two years of school teaching drove me to drugs," she chuckles. "And I stayed with the drugs 43 years, ten months and six days."

At 21, Geraldine bought a drugstore in Corona. She borrowed the down payment from a bank in a time when that kind of boldness from a woman was rare. "After I bought the store, I found out you had to be a registered pharmacist to own a drugstore, so I went to Wooster School of Pharmacy in Wichita, Kansas. My certificate is dated November 30, 1930." She was the fourth female pharmacist to register in the state of New Mexico.

Even with degenerating eyesight, she continued as the Du Bois Drug Store pharmacist until 1973. "Doctors aren't known for their fine handwriting," she recalls, "but as long as I could read the fine print, I could fill prescriptions. In all those years there were only two prescriptions I could not see to fill."

PHOTOS COURTESY PERKINS FAMILY

CLOCKWISE FROM ABOVE: Archie and Geraldine Perkins, Corona, New Mexico, mid-1970s. ▪ Geraldine at her homestead house, 1930s. ▪ Pharmacy school graduation in 1930. OPPOSITE: Geraldine in 2002.

In 1935, a young man who worked at the Corona Trading Company next door caught Geraldine's eye and they were soon married. Archie Perkins taught and coached at the Corona schools and tended the family ranching interests. They had two children, Sherrill (Bradford) and Rand, both of whom still live in Corona and ranch the family holdings.

Most of Geraldine's life has been dedicated to service organizations and improvement in education and health care in New Mexico. She spent many years on the committee of the Health System Agencies, an organization that regulated hospitals in New Mexico. She is a lifetime member of the local chapter of Beta Sigma Phi, and for 54 years a member of Pythian Sisters-Cedar Temple. She is the oldest member of Crown CowBelles, and is also a charter member of the Corona Presbyterian Church.

Geraldine fills her days with typing letters and listening to news magazines and books on tape. Her love of politics, sports and foreign affairs keeps her busy staying on top of current events. And she continues to be involved in the family ranch. "I'm still the boss. I can't write the checks but I'm the one who signs them."

Believing her mother was correct when she said it was important to stay smarter than your children, Geraldine works at it daily. "I wish I didn't think I needed eight hours of sleep. I don't have time to sleep. If I had more time I would walk more and type more."

Geraldine jokingly says she is looking into how much she can get paid for taking care of old people. She nods toward her daughter Sherrill who shares the home with her, and says: "She needs lots of taking care of. I may as well get paid for it."—*Julie Carter*

Essential companions and frequent characters, horses have long been the most valued and most admired creatures of a ranching life. But in their size and spirit, they could never be just pets, not all of them anyway. So those rewarded with their freedom in the spread of new technology have created a contradiction of conscience by over-grazing wildlands and herding around vital water sources. A society once so dependent on them can no longer afford all its horses, even when they are offered free. Where they still work and earn their keep is on the ranches.

A MULE NAMED SISTER CHICAGO RUNS WITH THE DUFURRENA RANCH MARES AND FOALS, DENIO, NEVADA.
PHOTO © LINDA DUFURRENA

TEXAS . SUMMER 1998

Collins Sayner, 99

A lot of crap in a hundred years.

Seven-year-old Darwin Sayner and his dog got lost on the family ranch in Tom Green County, Texas. He wandered around for a few hours, then found a cave beside a creek and holed up for the night. His dog barked and growled all night at the entrance to keep the varmints away. This was West Texas in 1885, so there were varmints aplenty, especially lobo wolves.

At dawn, the young fellow heard a rooster crow and followed the sound. He came to a homestead but couldn't pronounce his name so that the family could understand what he was saying. Finally they asked, "What's your daddy's brand?" Young Darwin scrawled out an SS in the dusty soil, and then they knew that Sam Sayner's son had shown up on their doorstep.

Sam came to Texas from England in the mid-1800s. He settled in Semperonius near Austin, married well, and then moved to the brush country north of San Angelo around 1882. He and his wife settled under a big oak tree to start improving their homestead land. Indians ran his horse off soon after they arrived, so the family slept in the brush at night so the Indians couldn't kill them and steal the babies. Sam registered the SS brand soon after homesteading. Today the brand belongs to Sam's grandson, Collins Sayner, who was born in 1899. The brand still adorns the flanks of Black Angus cattle on his ranch in Tennyson, Texas.

PHOTOS COURTESY COLLINS SAYNER

CLOCKWISE FROM ABOVE: A teenage Collins and friend, ca. 1913. ■ Collins in San Angelo, Texas, in 1940. ■ Today, at 99.

"My grandpa taught me how to ranch," Collins says. "My poppa had no interest in it, so grandpa taught me, and put me in charge of the ranch in about 1916. I've been ranching ever since. Hell, if I make it to the year 2000, I will have been on the ranch for a spread of three centuries. Think I'll make it. It's too damn expensive to die and I can't ask the Lord for any more than a hundred years."

Silver haired, the essence of dignity but full of fun, jokes and life, Collins is pretty blunt about what he has seen. "Hell, I've seen it all! You see a lot of crap in a hundred years; but you know, I have to say, every day since I was born has been a better day."

Collins often spins tales of cattle drives to the railhead in San Angelo, Texas, in 1918, and of riding on the train with the cattle to Fort Worth and getting a good price from the buyers when he was a lad of nineteen.

Collins got into the sheep business when the prices dropped on beef. He relives the problems he had with predators. "This country was crawling with wolves. I got a good pack of hounds and commenced to running them at night. I'd work all day and kill wolves at night. Must have killed hundreds before I finally got rid of them. Ain't missed 'em any!"

Collins still lives on the land where he was born. When he isn't working, he's on the phone with his broker, and he follows professional rodeo with a passion. He and his wife Maggie had no children, so he's teaching his niece Judy Bond how to ranch; and for the third century, the SS brand will still decorate the hides of Texas cattle.

"I was a pretty good cowboy," he says. "Even rodeoed for a while. Always had good horses. When I made money, I liked to spend it on Cadillac cars, Ford pickups, cigars, and good horses. I lived pretty fast; didn't fart around much. I still got a Cadillac and a pickup truck but I had to give up cigars and horses."—*J. Zane Walley*

Mary Flournoy, 96

Never plucked a chicken.

When she arrived in Likely, California, Mary Marshall figured it would be a short stay. That was more than 74 years ago. At age fourteen, after her mother died, Mary moved in with a sister in Red Bluff. She received her teacher training at Chico State College and was living with her sister and brother-in-law in Sacramento when she accepted a teaching job in Likely.

"I didn't know a soul," she says of traveling to the Modoc County hamlet by train in 1928 to begin work as a twenty-year-old schoolteacher. "I had never seen sagebrush and juniper. It was all gray. It was a little different than being in the valley. It was hard leaving my long-time friends, boyfriends." She grins. "You didn't think I had just one boyfriend, did you?"

All the way across the Madeline Plains she said, "I'm not going to stay here," but the conductor wasn't so sure. He told her, "I've taken a lot of teachers there, but I've never taken one back."

Mary remembers an intimidating sixteen-year-old eighth grader and a class accustomed to getting its way. "When I got here the message was, 'We run off the last teacher.'"

Now, at 96, Mary seldom strays far from what's become home. "It does grow on you," she admits of life in the wide-open spaces of Modoc County. "Now when I go places where there are lots of trees I feel closed in."

Two years after arriving in Likely, she married a local rancher, Kenneth Flournoy. "It wasn't love at first sight," she admits with a slight chuckle, "because I didn't like the country to begin with. I wasn't a very good ranch wife. I never milked a cow. I never plucked a chicken."

Others disagree. She helped as needed and, more importantly, kept the books for the ranch and raised two children. Mary has also made her mark on the community, with long involvements in many activities, including 45 years as a volunteer at the Warnerville Skilled Nursing Facility in Alturas, teaching English to Hispanic youths and mothers, and being a charter member of the Modoc County Cattlewomen.

PHOTOS © LEE JUILLERAT

COURTESY MARY FLOURNOY

CLOCKWISE FROM LEFT: Mary (this photo taken in 2002) thought she'd only be in Likely for a short stay. That was in 1928. ▪ Mary in the 1930s. ▪ Mary's brother-in-law Don is flanked by sons, from left, Dave, Billy and John. Members of the Flournoy family have been ranching in Likely, California, since 1871.

"I'll be a cattlewoman until I die," says Mary. "I eat beef all the time. We have to push it because we have way too many vegetarians."

Despite her age and her husband's death about twenty years ago, she continues to live in her tidy home that's just a short dirt-road drive from the Likely Land and Cattle Company operated by her nephews Billy, John and Dave Flournoy. Following her husband's death, they leased the 6,000-acre ranch for thirteen years until buying those lands about seven years ago.

"My husband always wanted to keep it in the family," says Mary, who regards her nephews as both family and business partners. Evidence of those bonds were made public when her nephews were jointly named Modoc County Cattlemen of the Year. Each received a belt buckle. John gave his to Mary. Although other plaques are put away and out of sight, that buckle has a prominent place in her living room.

"I have all kinds of plaques and this and that. I can't display them all; there are just too many. But those aren't what matters to me. I'd rather have the friendship of people." She keeps those friendships alive with weekly gatherings of the Likely Brunch Bunch, saying, "It's not really a gossip group." And she remembers dances at an old hall with supper at midnight and dancing to the sounds of The Happy Five Orchestra. "That was fancy. It was music, it wasn't rock. It was good dancing music."

Mary remains informed and interested in the business. She lives alone. "I read all the cattle magazines so I can keep up conversations with my friends. I don't sit around and feel sorry for myself. And," she adds with a smile, "I have three people who call me every night to see if I'm still alive."

—*Lee Juillerat*

BELOW: William Kittredge, a.k.a. Bill Kitt, rides Pretty Boy Floyd at Klamath Marsh, Oregon, in 1947. At the time of his death in 1958, he owned 19,000 head of raised (one-iron) cattle.
RIGHT: Bill and Maude Kittredge wedding photo, 1899.

Bill Kittredge was the kind of man who sat a horse like he did an executive office chair, and he did well at both. He knew cowhands got rowdy and that part of his job making the ranch work was to give them some time to be themselves. But everybody worked, and in those days, like now, were glad to have the chance.

ABOVE: Bill Kitt, center, with, from left, young Bill Kittredge, Jack Nicol, John Kittredge and Pat Kittredge in 1941. TOP LEFT: Ross Dollarhide was cow boss and one of the greatest buckaroos on the MC Ranch. He's fanning his hat for Tracy, and riding in style.

These images are from the book, "Bill Kitt: From Trail Driver to Cowboy Hall of Fame," by Jack Nicol and Amy Thompson, reprinted with permission. For more information, visit www.billkittbook.com.

Cowboys celebrate after a roundup at Silver Lake, Oregon, in the late '20s. Their boss Bill Kitt owned and operated ranches in three states. He owned 68,000 deeded acres. With leased land, he ran cattle on close to a million acres of high desert. These cowboys always left camp at a long run. Going 30 miles a day horseback, you couldn't start out in a walk. Sometimes it looked like a cavalry charge, with broncs that didn't buck in the corral, getting started after jumping the first sagebrush.

Harold Rogers, 100

A century of dancing and fishing.

When Harold Rogers was born on August 19, 1906, Teddy Roosevelt was president. Neither one of them was aware that they would share love of the outdoors and a downright passion for hunting and fishing all their lives.

Harold was born to Dave and Mary Alvira Rogers in Barron County, Wisconsin, in a humble farmhouse. He had four sisters and two brothers. In 1918, Dave joined his brother-in-law, George Edes, and moved out West to Oregon. He and the three boys drove out in their 1918 Model-T Ford. They had bought it brand new with proceeds from the sale of the homestead. Harold's mother and the girls came out by train. Harold had his twelfth birthday during that trip.

Highways were rare in those days so when they ran out of road, they simply crossed farmers' fields and pastures. Travelers who had done the same thing before the Rogers marked the route with yellow paint on rocks and trees to show those coming later which direction to head in. The yellow objects became their road map.

The two families settled in Yoncalla, Oregon, where Harold's dad bought a house for his family and a livery stable to earn his living. Harold remembers his first job: "I was about fourteen or fifteen, working as a farmhand, haying, harvesting crops and milking for one dollar a day plus room and board."

Harold was drafted into the Army Air Corps during World War II. He served in Italy, Africa and India until he was discharged on September 5, 1945. "I couldn't wait to pick up my fishing pole and deer rifle, and head for the hills."

Harold met and married Martha Lee on August 8, 1947. They have been married 60 years. Their honeymoon was a four-day weekend, with Harold taking two days off work at the mill. "I didn't dream that he would take his fishing pole on our honeymoon!"

Martha says. "That should have been my first clue as to what life would be

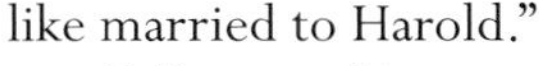

like married to Harold."

Following thirteen years in the lumber mills, Harold went to work for the U.S. Forest Service as a mechanic in Toketee. He retired in 1972 at the age of 65. "Then I was able to do things that I really wanted to do."

He worked as a deckhand for Curly Leach, who owned a fishing boat in Winchester Bay. Curly had only one arm and Harold was hired to pull the fish in. He then worked for a pack station owned by Bud Sanders and Gordon Summers. They

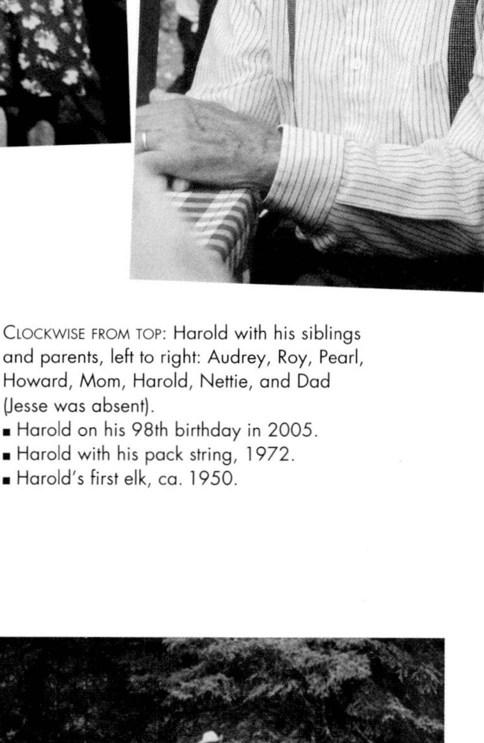

PHOTOS COURTESY ROGERS FAMILY

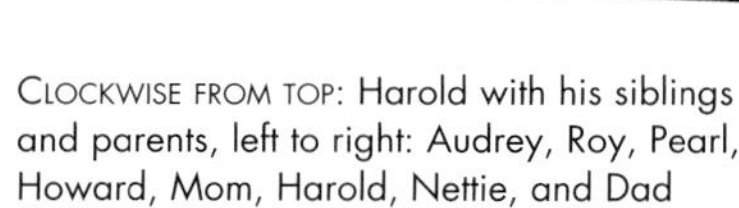

CLOCKWISE FROM TOP: Harold with his siblings and parents, left to right: Audrey, Roy, Pearl, Howard, Mom, Harold, Nettie, and Dad (Jesse was absent).
- Harold on his 98th birthday in 2005.
- Harold with his pack string, 1972.
- Harold's first elk, ca. 1950.

took clients on elk-hunting trips, packing into the Eagle Cap wilderness area. Harold loaded the mules with supplies for the weeklong stay and made sure everybody was comfortable, and, hopefully, that each client could take back an elk. One day he told Bud, "I don't want to stay in camp. I want to get everybody set up and go hunting on my own." Bud agreed. "I got them settled in and then took two mules and a saddle horse and took off." He went about fifteen miles and stayed about four days, bringing back a three-point elk. He was around 70 years old at that time.

He and Martha loved to dance and never missed a fiddler's jam session at the Sutherlin Senior Center, dancing up a storm until Martha had back surgery and couldn't dance anymore. But that didn't stop Harold! Martha would sit on the sidelines while Harold whirled and twirled all the ladies, never missing a dance tune.

On his 99th birthday, the Senior Center gave him a party. The finale of the afternoon was that all the ladies lined up with a dollar bill in their hands, and after dancing with Harold they tucked their dollar bill in his shirt pocket. When it was all over, he brags, "I made twenty bucks!"

For the past several years, the family has had a reunion/birthday for him. On his 98th, he and his grandson Jan Rogers and his nephew Bruce Ramberg went fishing for tuna, an all-day trip on the ocean. On his 99th, they went on another all-day trip with Harold reeling in a 64-pound halibut. And on his 100th birthday, nephew Bruce took him trout fishing on Foster Lake near Sweet Home, Oregon.

One of Harold's pet peeves is his driver's license. In 2002, he went to the Department of Motor Vehicles to renew it. He was 95. They renewed it for eight more years! He still grumbles that "they know I'm not going to live that long. All they wanted was to get that money from me."—*Ginny Paseman*

OREGON . FALL 2003

Maxine Loosely Kizer, 80

When Maxine (wearing bow) was born on April 14, 1922, Fort Klamath was a bustling community with dairies, dances and potlucks. Winters seemed to last forever. It was during one of those that Maxine was born, on the ranch her family has owned since 1873 and where she still lives.

"Even though it was April," she says. "I always heard my mother talk about that horrible snow, with hardpack that the horses used to be able to run on top of. My mother had planned to go to the hospital, but we had a real bad storm." Her father, Raymond, bought the ranch after his 1917 marriage to Willeska Roberts, a Fort Klamath schoolteacher. Maxine was the third of six children. "Life wasn't always easy growing up on a dairy ranch during the Depression years," she says. "I remember many cold winter nights when we kids were left to mind the house while Mother helped Daddy with the milking. Sometimes after a storm, it'd be maybe two months before we got out."—*Lee Juillerat*

IDAHO . WINTER 2004

Tom Hall, 80

"I like the cowboy way of living," says 80-year-old Tom. "I try to ride a horse about every day. I feel good about just being on a horse." He's never been to much of anywhere outside Idaho, except the Pacific during World War II and three years in Nevada as a hired hand, "but my heart was always here. Three days away and I'm so homesick I can't stand it. This ranch is all I know."

Neighboring ranches in this remote area on the road to rugged Bruneau Canyon, a lariat throw from Buckaroo Ditch in Idaho's sprawling Owyhee County, have mostly gone under. "In 1974, we got 92 cents a pound for cattle and bought a new Chevy pickup for $5,000. You tell me who's makin' money. If you're in the cattle business to make money, you're in the wrong business. We're just a small operation—a few cattle and horses and some hay and other crops. We don't try to keep up with the Joneses. It's more fun meeting them on the way back."

—*Tim Woodward*

WYOMING . SPRING 1994

Charlie Thomas, 88

Born April 1, 1905, on the family ranch at Fort Bridger, Wyoming, Charlie Thomas has spent his 88 years involved with livestock and working with horses. As a youngster, he rode a little black mule that could jump over any gate, but that mule had an ornery streak. "I never had to get off to open a gate," Charlie says, "but I had to tie him to a post to get on or off his back!"

Charlie herded sheep at Piedmont, Wyoming, for ten years, learning self-sufficiency, responsibility, and at the same time saving money for a down payment on a ranch. He became an excellent cook, famous for sourdough biscuits. "I took care of sheep instead of cows," he laughs, "because cowboys got $30 a month, and sheepherders got $40."—*Heather Smith Thomas*

You could run to a place like Wyoming intending to get lost, but it might not be long before you were just too proud not to share it, both with your own family and with neighbors who wanted as much to be found again.

AFTERNOON THUNDERSTORM, THUNDER BASIN NATIONAL GRASSLAND, WYOMING. PHOTO © LARRY ANGIER

Cora Lees Cole, 85

Too poor for beef.

At 85 years old, Cora Lees Cole no longer thinks twice about having a hamburger. But as a youngster, beef was a rare event at her family's table because they were too poor.

Cora was named after Cora, Wyoming, the town where she was born. Her parents had moved by team and wagon to the cooler climate of Wyoming from Kansas in 1903 when her father, Chester "Chet" Lees, was diagnosed with epilepsy.

Chet was a jack-of-all-trades. Over the years he worked as a cowboy, on the railroad, carrying freight and in construction. But because of his epileptic attacks, the children often had to accompany him in his work and when he suffered a seizure, he was usually laid off. It made for a hard existence without assurance of steady employment.

Nevertheless, Cora has fond memories of her childhood with her parents and five siblings. They lived in a one-room, twenty-foot pole tent with a cookstove in the middle. At night they slept on homemade beds, side by side on the hard-packed dirt floor. For meals, Cora's mother Maud often ground sage chicken and rabbit into homemade sausage. They ate it with rice and mixed it with milk, vegetables, "or whatever." But Cora couldn't enjoy the cream skimmed from the milk, because that was sold for grocery money.

They lived in a one-room, twenty-foot pole tent with a cookstove in the middle. They slept on a hard-packed dirt floor.

When she was six, she walked four miles to school each way. In the winter, when the snow was four feet deep, all the children were pulled to school by horse and sleigh. After school, Cora milked, churned butter and, at age nine, made biscuits by herself for the entire hay crew.

At the end of World War I, Cora's family moved to Esterbrook, Wyoming. Her older sister had married Harold "Slim" Tennyson, who was homesteading. Chet, Maud and their children moved onto his place.

At fourteen, Cora married Elvin "Red" Cole and had her first of six children. Red was a cowboy and ranch hand, and after several years, they began to work and live on the land they leased. Red worked odd jobs herding sheep and cattle and contracting hay. Cora frequently worked beside him mowing, raking and baling.

About this time, they had saved enough money to buy a few sheep and cattle. They went boom and bust twice as cattle prices fluctuated. The worst incident was the drought of 1930. With no feed for the cattle, the government offered to buy cows from ranchers for $13 a head—dramatically less than the $60 market price before the drought. Cora and Red drove the cows out by the railroad, where government workers shot and buried the cows. Despite the Great Depression, no one was allowed to eat the slaughtered animals and only the calves remained. The family survived on veal.

"I can't stand veal now," says Cora with a gleam in her eye. "Red meat is better."—*Ann Symonds*

PHOTOS COURTESY COLE FAMILY

ABOVE: In 1938, the Coles get ready to go to a rodeo. Left to right: Eugene, Red, Stanley, Bernice, Betty, Lyle, Norma and Cora.
LEFT: Four generations of Coles in front of the blacksmith shop in Cora, Wyoming. Left to right: Cora's daughter Norma, Cora, Cora's grandson Gary, and one of her numerous great-grandchildren.

Edsil Runyan, 80

Coyotes thicker than jackrabbits.

Edsil Runyan's face has about as many gullies and arroyos as the Chihuahuan Desert where he has lived and ranched for 80 years. It's not a gentle land, but a southern New Mexico land of parched, fiery hot summers and howling winter blue northers. Folks who spend a lifetime here have the dry rolling plains and winds etched deeply in their faces.

ABOVE: Edsil and a couple of months' worth of hides.
BELOW: Edsil and one of those good horses that could cover 40 miles a day in a lope.

PHOTOS COURTESY EDSIL RUNYAN

Edsil's father, Tom Runyan, was one of those weathered cowboys. In 1882, he trailed a herd of 7,000 cattle bearing the famous YO brand from Kerrville, Texas, to southern New Mexico. Tom rode for the YO three years, took his pay in cattle, and then started his own spread on open range. Tom married Bonnie C. Wilburn, a chipper lass who walked behind a covered wagon from Fort Worth, Texas, to Hope, New Mexico, around 1890.

All Edsil's wrinkles kinda tip up toward the brim of his well-oiled hat as he remembers his parents and the old days. "I wore out three saddles, and I do mean plum wore out, in 36 years on this ranch. My brothers and I worked it a-horseback. Right after we bought it, Dave got called to the Army and was gone for four or five years. That left me here. I couldn't hire nobody 'cause all the men were in the service."

Edsil managed to find an old-timer to help him out for two weeks but remembers, "He was so slow that it took him seven years to finish two weeks' work." There was no time for fun. "Got so damn busy working that I didn't make it to town for thirteen months. My brother J.B. would bring me a sack of split peas and 'taters every month or so; elsewise I just lived on beef."

Sheep were raised along with Edsil's cattle. Huge losses of lambs to coyotes, eagles and bobcats made that a rough go. "The coyotes," he says, "were thicker than jackrabbits. We had to fight 'em day and night. Reckon we killed hundreds of them, but there was one...the one I called that old son of a bitch...that really hurt us."

He had a ten-section ewe pasture with about 1,500 head in it. "In a year's time, the coyotes killed over 500 lambs. Me and the government hunter tracked them to the den and found a litter of pups. We set about twenty traps around the den and caught the bitch first night. The old dog come in the next night, worked his way around all them traps and left with a pup."

That coyote came back every year for four years with a new bitch. "I could trap the female, but he always got away. Got so I could recognize his track, so I loaded up a packhorse and commenced to trail him. When I had his route down, I put a trap in it and caught him. I figure he and his whelps killed over 2,000 sheep. He sure was smart."

Edsil looks sad when he tells this story, like he hated to lose all those sheep, but maybe it hurt him to kill that clever coyote he matched wits with for four years because Edsil appreciates smart animals. But he lights up when he recalls, "Horses were our transportation, and they had to be good'uns. When you left out of that corral, you'd better leave in a lope 'cause going to the west side of the ranch was eighteen miles. Then the horse had to come back! Lot of the riding was with a packhorse to haul fencing supplies. I strung 182 miles of net wire trying to keep coyotes out; 65 miles of that was eighteen-inch apron wire so they couldn't dig under."

On top of the varmint hunting and fencing, Edsil had another little problem. "The ranch Dave and I bought was property the government had foreclosed on, and the fellow who got evicted was upset. He'd park his car on the road and holler, 'There's gonna be another killing!' His daddy had bushwhacked my uncle a few years back, so I took the hint and bought a six-shooter, strapped it on, and wore it everywhere. When he'd come up the road and start yelling 'bout a killing, I'd just slap my gun and grin. The old boy give it up after three years and stopped coming around."

Edsil is still ranching, but his stock is sure different. He's trout ranching alongside the Peñasco River in the foothills of the Sacramento Mountains. He keeps his hand in sheep and meat-goat ranching by helping his son and nephew with their spreads. He's still going from daylight to dark and eating red meat.

"I gotta cut that meat out," he chuckles. "Why a 97-year-old fellow up the river just died and he ate it every day. No doubt that's what killed him!"

—*J. Zane Walley*

CALIFORNIA . FALL 2005

Oscar Haise, 89

Beef, beans, biscuits and gravy.

PHOTOS COURTESY HAISE FAMILY

CLOCKWISE FROM TOP LEFT: Georgia, Oscar, Jackie and Roger Haise in 1947. ▪ Oscar with Georgia. ▪ Delighted to be back in the saddle on a good sorrel horse with some fine cattle to work.

Oscar Haise, the youngest of four, was born in Russell, Kansas, to Edwin and Louisa Haise on January 15, 1915. His parents pioneered in Crowley County, Colorado, when Oscar was three.

At twelve, Oscar started helping a neighbor, Bob Wright, who had cattle and horses. Horses were the boy's first love, and he had a way with the colts. There were no fences across the plains at that time, and he would ride the colts until they would respond to the reins, wherever they might run.

While in school, Oscar drove the school bus for a year and a half. "Then Colorado decided that drivers needed to be licensed. I would have been old enough for a license in January of the next year—only two months later. I asked a teacher to fill in for me until I could get a license, but he refused, so I lost that job."

The Depression was especially hard on that country because of the drought and dust storms. After Oscar graduated from high school in 1932, he would break three colts and receive one additional colt as pay. He helped trail cattle north and south looking for grass. One winter in the San Luis Valley, Oscar lived in a shack with the roof and sides so loose they had to shovel dust off the beds and floor every night before turning in.

"We'd read for a while before sleeping," Oscar says, "and the dust would drift in on the book so we had to blow it off before we could turn the page. We lived on beans, coffee, beef and biscuits, with dried apricots thrown in for dessert."

During the Depression years, Oscar went to the State Penitentiary in Canyon City, where a former neighbor was warden, to get bits, spurs, and hatbands for trading goods. He would layer the hatbands from largest to the tiniest on his hat. When someone admired one of the bands, he'd say: "What do you have to trade?" In this manner, he was able to get knives and tack for further trades. He would also trade horses, sometimes getting a cow or another horse, but rarely cash. Money was scarce. He went to Aspen to help a rancher put up hay. "I saddled up my horse and took off for Gunnison, Colorado. There were still some snowdrifts up high on those mountains, but the horse and I made it to Gunnison, where I sold her and got a ride on a trainload of cattle headed east. That is the way I returned home."

In 1937, Oscar met Georgia, the love of his life. They married in January 1938 after two months of dating because he couldn't afford the frequent trips to see her. Making a living in those days was tough in Colorado so, with their daughter, they moved to California where Oscar's older sister lived. Georgia cooked while Oscar cowboyed. They were on the Santa Margarita Ranch when it was bought out by the government to make Camp Pendleton. They worked for Newhall Land and Cattle Company until 1944, when Oscar took the job as brand inspector in Modoc County, California.

He worked as brand inspector until 1950, then he went back to work on a ranch near Gerlach, Nevada. Several other jobs followed. Eventually, an opportunity to own a ranch in Arkansas presented itself. They lived there for 22 years until Georgia passed away in 1995. They had by then retired and sold the property.

In February 1996, Oscar got in his car and drove to Likely, California, to visit with his son-in-law Ken and daughter Jackie McGarva. A huge snowstorm occurred the next day. Oscar went back to work helping to calve and feed cows, delighted to be back in the saddle again. He is still helping to feed, riding his old horse whenever the need arises and moving cattle around.

Oscar tries to visit Arkansas for a few days or weeks each year to see son Roger and many good friends. His favorite meal is still "beef, beans, biscuits and gravy."

—*Jackie McGarva*

Brownie Ford, 89

Mostly fakin' it.

There is a vast difference between working cattle in the bogs of Louisiana and the brush country of Texas. "Well, hell," says 89-year-old Brownie Ford, "anybody can see a cow all the way over yonder and get around and drive her wherever yer goin' in Texas, but down in them bogs it's treacherous."

Thomas Edison "Brownie" Ford has run cattle in the bayou for many years, and says for that kind of work he prefers a horse over a mule, "because he's got more foot size and he don't bog as quick. A mule uses all his energy pullin' his feet outta' the ground."

Ranching in the bogs presents other problems, and Brownie has overcome them all. "They calls that country rich vegetation," he says with a strong southern drawl. "What they mean is that everthang down there got a damn thorn in it. It'll either sting ya', bite cha' or kick ya'." Wearing rubber boots with spurs on to get around in that country, Brownie can't always buck nature, and he's lost his share of calves in the swamps. "Alligators been known to knock a pretty good yearlin' off in the water. It's just how the good Lord fixed 'em to make a livin'."

Brownie has not always been in Louisiana. He has worked all over the country in rodeos, oil fields, and Wild West shows. He even roached mules. "In my narrow category of endeavor," he says with a twinkle in his eyes, "I'd go to a horse and mule barn anywhere and go to work." He could "barber on a mule" and fix a tail and trim a mane to where the mule looked a whole lot better. But he admits to having problems with skinny mules. "If you weren't careful roaching their tails, they'd look like the end of a coach-whip snake."

In the Wild West shows, Brownie worked for Indian Joe Key and M.L. Clark & Sons Great Combined Wagon Show. He was a horse jingler and he took care of the stock. "We didn't have any trucks or trailers and so we moved from town to town pulling wagons by horse and mules. I wasn't the foreman," he chuckles. "I was the man that done the work." He didn't make a lot of money as a jingler but Brownie could count on getting a meal. "We'd get beans and coffee and they'd have some kinda meat almost ever' meal."

Along the way, Brownie married and split up a couple of times, but his third-wife Cody has been with him for more than 30 years. It appears that she's in it for the long haul. He'd been tramping all over the country, and met Cody while singing in a bar in Memphis. "If it ain't married," she told her saloon boss, "I'm gonna marry it."

Brownie was born in 1904, and his ranching days began before the start of the first world war. He was only nine years old when he quit school to work for his uncle in Oklahoma. They ran what Brownie calls "long yearlin's"—little steers—in the Jack Oak country. "It was hard country, where vegetation didn't have no strength in it." Though Brownie didn't receive a formal education, he learned life's lessons through firsthand experience. "I got hard knowledge," he says, "and hard knowledge don't come easy. I know. I learned to ride buckin' horses and there was many a fall doin' that learnin'."

C.J. HADLEY PHOTOS

Brownie Ford has been buckarooing in the swamps for a lot of years. When he's not wearing rubber boots with spurs on, he likes singing to a crowd, especially if he's backed up by a good picker.

Today Brownie still ranches, eats meat all the time, and even does a little singing. In fact, he's won some awards from the Library of Congress and the Smithsonian Institution for his music. He even received a letter from Ronald and Nancy Reagan, although he says, "It was just a li'l ole note." One thing's for sure, Brownie doesn't hide the fact that he's no musician. He claims to know only three chords on the guitar and likes to play with a pro. He admits he always needs something in his hands, often a cigarette. "I need a wheel horse, as Bob Wills used to say, somebody to carry me, because I'm mostly fakin' it."

—*Jason Wallace*

SALEM LUTHERAN CHURCH, KANSAS. PHOTO © LARRY ANGIER

Out on the plains of Kansas, the great fields of wheat and grains form an ocean with waves rolling in the breeze. Yet the roads cut through in mostly straight lines section by section. And if you were patient and watched carefully, you could always find that one spot somewhere near the center where the people invested first their faith and, as often, their joy.

KANSAS . SUMMER 2005

Gilbert Knipp, 90

Looking for a job that paid.

Born a son of the soil in 1914 at Ellinwood, Kansas, Gilbert Knipp's family, like so many of their German ancestors, longed for bigger and better farms. In the late 1920s, they rented 1,000 acres of grassland near Scott City, a stone's throw from the Colorado border, planting wheat and barley along with their dreams of prosperity.

Upon his high school graduation in 1932, the *Hutchinson News* offered Gilbert a job working on its daily newspaper. "My high school English teacher recommended me for the job," Gilbert says. But Hutchinson was 200 miles away and there was no money for auto gas or a train ticket. "No one had any money then. So it was not as hard as you might think, turning down the chance to leave the farm."

He worked alongside his dad, trying to coax a living off the land. Seven years and only one successful harvest later, Gilbert took his new bride Barbara to Wichita where jobs actually paid money. Barbara was a city girl who saw her father shepherd trolley cars around Wichita from sunup to sundown. This would be a fresh start for the young couple trying to shake years of "Dirty '30s" dust and memories.

Gilbert succeeded at selling Hoover vacuum cleaners, Sears refrigerators and design work at the Steerman (later purchased by Boeing) aviation plant. Wichita was quickly becoming the "Air Capital" of Kansas.

"I made more money selling vacuums and building airplanes," Gilbert says, "than I ever did farming."

When World War II erupted he was building trainers for the U.S. Army Air Corps. Gilbert spent the war years in production planning, Barbara in accounting, all the while hearing the farm and ranch calling their names. Times were better on the farm now and a hungry post-war world needed to be fed.

In 1945, they returned to western Kansas and partnered with Gilbert's dad and his brother. The agricultural cycle had swung back in their favor with profitable prices and good weather. They were one of the first to have irrigation wells and the sandy-loam soil responded with bountiful crops of wheat, grain sorghum, corn, sugar beets, millet and buffalo grass.

They built a small feedlot, custom feeding cattle and building a purebred Angus herd. A 1958 blizzard buried the feedlot in snowdrifts taller than the house. "It was a mess," Gilbert recalls. "There were cattle scattered throughout the country. It was spring before we found some of them." He borrowed a Caterpillar tractor to dig out the silage pit, struggling to feed the cattle in the worst storm to ever hit the area.

There was always work to be done and for that they had a ready work force—six children, three boys and three girls. Gilbert bought out his brother and rode good times and bad, always willing to try something new. He grew certified seed for the now-defunct Rudy Patrick Seed Company, hiring migrant laborers to hand hoe the fields.

When the cattle market tanked in the early 1970s, Gilbert fought back by crossbreeding his Angus cows with Charolais bulls. "The Angus cows were great milkers," Gilbert says, "and the Charolais bulls produced huge, gray-colored calves that were quite a sight out there on the prairie. It was not unusual to have an 80- or 90-pound birth weight on the calves."

Pure joy entered his heart when he saddled his trusted Appaloosa gelding and patrolled the pastures, checking on his ever-expanding cattle herd. "Old Blue Boy was ornery as the devil, but we had an understanding," Gilbert says. "When it was time to bring the cattle in, he knew what to do."

Surviving decades of fluctuating prices and difficult weather conditions required Gilbert to fine-tune his sense of humor. At his 90th birthday party he was asked the secret to a long life. "I'm not telling you because you probably wouldn't believe me!"—*Sam Knipp*

PHOTOS COURTESY KNIPP FAMILY

CLOCKWISE FROM TOP: Gilbert playing cowboy on his ranch in the late 1940s. ▪ Riding his ornery Appaloosa named Old Blue Boy. ▪ Barbara and Gilbert happily traded city for farm.

George Moore, 91

Fighting Germans took a really long time.

PHOTOS COURTESY GEORGE MOORE

© ROBIN SACHAU

CLOCKWISE FROM TOP: Port of Entry Corrals on the Mexico/U.S. border, Campo, California, August 1937. Herds purchased in Mexico were driven to Las Huntas to be dipped, then trailed to Campo and weighed. ■ George holds a frame with the medals he was awarded for his military service during World War II. He was a survey sergeant in the renowned 3rd Infantry Division. ■ Marie and George Moore, Holbrook, Arizona, 1951.

George Moore was raised by his father who died when George was just eighteen. "I used my inheritance to purchase a boxcar of cattle," George says. "Around $600 for 30 cows."

George recalls that Brawley, California, was the "big hangout" for Imperial Valley cowboys looking for work. "The Silver Moon Café and Bar was the best place to be in—four dollars and one meal was the going rate for day work."

George worked off and on for a cattleman named Tom Reed, but soon Uncle Sam called. George was inducted into the Army on December 1, 1941, and spent 33 months overseas. Remarkably, at Anzio, Italy, the 3rd Infantry Division fought off three German divisions. When reminded of this feat, George laughs, "Yeah, but it took us a really long time." The division was immortalized in the 1950 movie, "To Hell and Back," starring Audie Murphy, its most-decorated member.

In 1945, George returned to the work that he loved. He returned to California, and in 1951 he married a pretty Brawley waitress named Marie Gillum. "She was always happy, a good housekeeper and an excellent cook. She really knew how to put on a good spread."

Their first home was in a tin house on the Rocking Chair Ranch in Holbrook, Arizona. He and Marie moved there to work for old friend Tom Reed for 25 percent of the net profit. George branded every fourth calf. "Prices fell from 50 cents a pound down to twenty cents a pound, and the following year all the way down to thirteen cents a pound," he says. Tom felt bad that cattle prices had gone to heck, so he sold George 111 heifers that George kept for a few years. Tom had written a contract for George on the back of an envelope and wanted him to stay in Holbrook, but George says, "I always liked handling my own money, so I decided to move on."

Over the years the Moores lived on ranches in Arizona, New Mexico, Texas, Idaho, Nevada, Oregon and California. Later, George threw in with Columbia River Cattle on a deal right on the Columbia River near Clatskanie, Oregon. It was quite an experience. "The cattle had to be barged over to the islands that were a part of the ranch." The cowboys rode over in a separate boat while their saddle horses, tied with neck ropes, would swim alongside. The area's 75 inches of rain made the tides rise swiftly, and snowpack runoff only added to the problems. George says, "I never liked the water that much, and I kept a tide book with me at all times." The ranches were eventually sold off in pieces—some to Burt Lancaster.

One day Marie announced that Burl Byrd had offered George a job in a small feedlot (averaging 18,000 head) in Calipatria, California, for $1,700 a month with benefits. "It didn't take me long to think that over," says George. So they rolled up their beds, moved back to the Imperial Valley and stayed there for seven years before returning to Nevada in 1980.

George became an avid collector of bits, spurs, and rawhide and braided gear. Present-day quality craftsmen like Al Tietjen and Eduardo Grijalva have something hanging on his wall. George's favorite piece of gear is a hair rope made for him in 1950 by Ralph Brown, the boss at the Mission Viejo Ranch near San Juan Capistrano. "Ralph was the best cowboy and cowman I ever saw." His lifelong gear collection has been displayed at the Pioneer Museum & Cultural Center in Imperial, California, and some pieces can be seen at D Bar M Saddlery in Reno.

As you might guess, George's odometer has a lot of miles on it. He still travels to select ranches and cowboy events to display his junk, as he calls it. His booth, consisting of the tailgate of his pickup and a couple of card tables, is usually crowded with cowboys.—*Robin Sachau*

Joe Smith, 87

Quitting when they pat my face with a shovel.

When Joe Smith answers the door he is wearing a new bandage-type cast on his left hand and forearm. At his age, one might suspect the damage done was by a fall of some sort. His explanation makes it clear the only falling was done by a runaway bull. Just days before, Joe had been teaching some neighborly manners to a bull that refused to stay in the pasture where it belonged. A few cowboy maneuvers that were meant to educate the bull but were a little foreign to his roan horse caused a cowboy-roping wreck. Joe ended up with eighteen stitches in his hand and some pulled ligaments. Shaking that off as business as usual, he reports that the bull has learned to stay home.

Even at 87, Joe does not have any plans for stopping. Not working is a foreign concept for him. "When I quit will be when they pat my face with a shovel as they cover me up. I don't know any other way."

Born the fifth of seven children on September 7, 1919, in Seymour, Texas, Joe went to work right out of high school at the historic Slaughter Ranch near Whiteface. "I quit riding bulls and started riding broncs because every time I saddled up at the ranch I got practice."

At a 1940 Levelland, Texas, rodeo, a bronc named High Lonesome sunfished and fell, as was his habit to do, and 21-year-old Joe ended up with a crushed right foot and leg. "That bronc crippled three cowboys before they pulled him out of the bucking string."

© JULIE CARTER

PHOTO COURTESY JOE SMITH

ABOVE: Joe recalls the day of the wreck aboard a bronc named High Lonesome, when he was just 21. RIGHT: Joe and one of his good horses at the Double H's Ranch near Datil, New Mexico, in 1995.

The accident laid Joe up for two months and kept him from reporting for duty during World War II. Pop Bettis, a legendary Texas panhandle saddle maker, took Joe into his business and taught him to build saddles. Joe stayed there for four years and during that time he married Dolly Williams, an Amarillo bookkeeper. They were together 27 years, had two girls and lost a baby son. During those years Joe hung up his bronc saddle and started team roping.

In 1947, Joe went to work for the Jay Taylor Cattle Company, which operated five ranches and two feedlots. He retired in the '80s from his manager's job but remained on the payroll as a consultant. He helped with spring brandings and fall shipping until 1999.

Joe has had both knees replaced and an arm rebuilt. Except for the many broken bones and old scars, he is as healthy as his young horses. He has perfectly normal blood pressure, still has his own teeth, wears no hearing aids or glasses and takes no medications. "If I had new arms and legs, I'd be in good shape."

Joe has buried three wives in his 87 years, cancer taking each of them. His second wife of seventeen years, Martha Myers, died in 1987. In 1990 he married Lucille Jones who lost her battle with leukemia in 2004, after sixteen years of marriage.

Today he is still working. He rides cutting horses for a local trainer. A normal day is eight to ten head of horses to saddle and ride. Last March a horse bucked pretty hard with him and, although he rode the horse, Joe pulled some ligaments in his leg. "I told Wes [the trainer], 'Catch this S.O.B., I gotta get off.'"

Joe still builds saddles, chaps, and assorted cowboy tack. He currently has six saddle orders to fill. "Back when I was doing this full-time I'd make six saddles a week. I don't know how people just sit in the house."

Looking back, Joe is clear about his life. Grinning, he declares, "I wouldn't take anything for my experience, but I damn sure don't want to do it all again."—*Julie Carter*

UTAH . SUMMER 2009

Gerald 'Jed' Cook, 90

On every jump that horse bit my stirrup.

When folks ask Jed Cook if he has lived in Ibapah his whole life, he answers, "Well, I was born in Lehi, Utah, September 16, 1918, and as soon as I had my first bowel movement, they brought me to Deep Creek. I've been here ever since."

Ibapah and Deep Creek are one and the same, an isolated valley in the western desert of Utah. Jed is a second-generation cowboy. His father Will and three brothers came to Deep Creek in 1898. They were cowboys, musicians and adventurers, and had a reputation throughout Tooele County for their ability with horses.

Fred Boyd and his mother lived on the other side of the mountain from Ibapah. They came to town to get groceries. They went to Devine's store with their team and wagon, loaded their supplies and were heading home, going down Overland Canyon. "We saw this string of riders coming up the canyon," Fred told Jed. "It was the four Cook boys. They all had musical instruments tied on their saddles. Will had a bass fiddle tied on the horn of a little mustang and his fiddle on the back. Abe had his fiddle and John had his banjo."

Mrs. Boyd offered a meal and afterwards they played their instruments. Jed learned to play harmonica, piano and accordion.

Jed's father died when he was nine. The dying man's advice to his son was: "Don't smoke, don't drink, be kind to others and, above all, be honest." He gave Jed his gold pocket watch and then he was gone.

When Jed was fourteen, his brother-in-law, Sammy Littledyke, sold some horses to the Cleveland Ranch at the south end of Spring Valley. Sam gave Jed $10 to trail the horses 40 miles from Deep Creek to the Cleveland Ranch. It was raining and snowing when he arrived, so he stayed for several days. While heading back, it began to storm again and got dark. He let the horse have its rein and finally discovered where he was when he got above Eight Mile Ranch. The trip took about twelve hours.

Jed married his sweetheart, Joyce Parrish. She was the daughter of Wade Parrish, a local sheep rancher. They had four children: Joycelyn, Marylin, David, and Les. They bought the old Kelley place and also ran his mother's ranch. They raised kids, cattle, horses, alfalfa, oats, and a giant garden. Jed was proud to be able to brand cattle without any "extra help getting in the way." He would start the cattle drive at daybreak, then string them out through the hills to his mother's place. He'd get 300 cows and their calves corralled, separated, castrated, marked and branded in two to three days. Joyce would drive up with a pot of beans in the afternoons.

Jed's always had a natural gift with horses. He likes the ones that are a little "broncy." One of his best horses was named Ol' Pinto.

"Ol' Pinto was a piebald sorrel, lanky with no belly. He would for no apparent reason drop his head out of sight and go to buckin'." Jed adds, "That horse had such athletic ability that every jump he'd make, he'd reach around and hit your stirrup with the bit and the next jump he'd do it again, on the opposite side." Jed's horses are well reined, cowy, well mannered (except they might buck a little), handy, and good travelers.

He also has a fondness for mules. "Fitzgerald would jump in the back of the pickup truck like a dog." He bought a pretty registered mule with a fancy name and was showing her to his cousin Leatha. "Something spooked the mule and she went to buckin'." Jed had his old Hamley saddle on. He stayed on for quite some time but she finally lost him. His spurs' rowel marks remain in the seat of that old saddle as proof he was there. He was 77 at the time.

Jed's pelvis, ribs, hip, knee, and femur have all been busted up by horses. He sets off the metal detectors in all the airports because of the screws and pins he carries in his legs. Arthritis is also creeping in but it doesn't slow him down. He finds the saddle with the flattest cantle so he can slide his leg over. He uses a rock to mount his horse on his property on the mountain. The rock stands eighteen inches high and overlooks a steep slope. Jed puts his horse on the low side, climbs on the rock, then onto the horse.

PHOTOS COURTESY JED COOK

CLOCKWISE FROM TOP: Jed and Ol' Pinto, ca. 1953. ▪ Jed on roan mare, June 2008. It still takes a good cowboy to keep up with him. ▪ Jed riding Bishop mule, 1992.

On his 90th birthday, Jed, his grandson Ethan and daughter Marylin rode to the Queen of Sheba mine. He told stories of how the guys built the big cabin and constructed the mill and mine, all by hand and horse. He told of how they built a pulley system to haul the ore from the top of the mountain to the bottom.

It still takes a good cowboy to keep up with him. One of his favorite sayings when he describes someone who is a pretty rider is, "She sits up there straighter than a string."—*Marylin Linares*

FIREWEED-LINED TRAIL TO LITTLE MOLAS LAKE, SAN JUAN MOUNTAINS, COLORADO. PHOTO © LARRY ANGIER

The Front Range of the Rockies challenged you first to find this reward. Ahead lay even greater peaks still shoulder to shoulder in snow. But this was spring in the high country of Colorado, and your heart cried out for now, stop.

Dorcas Lowery, 83

Outlaw granny broke heifers to ride.

"I was born June 3, 1922," says Dorcas Hall Lowery. "My daddy homesteaded in the Four Corners area, then we rode the Galloping Goose to the main railroad line, then on to Missouri. I had rheumatic fever at two years old. We came back to Colorado in the spring of 1928. We bought 360 acres in Utah. I grew up there. It was all open range then. I didn't have a horse so I broke a heifer to ride. I have a picture of my dad on her."

Dorcas' father traded five shocks of corn for a turquoise bracelet for her. When she was nine, he traded a pocket watch for a mustang. "She turned out to be a great cutting horse. I was not allowed to have a saddle. I would ride miles from home in the canyons."

When she was ten, her mother got sick. Snow and mud was bad; roads were never graded in the winter. "My dad and a neighbor got Mama to Dove Creek to the doctor. I was alone for a week with horses and cows to feed and water, hogs and chickens to care for. I had to milk the cows and cut wood for the stove. I wasn't late one time for school. Now they call the cops if you leave a ten-year-old alone."

Dorcas says they always had plenty of meat, milk, butter, eggs, canned fruit and vegetables—but no money during the Depression.

"It was common to see many men in town with six-guns strapped to their hips. Colorado was still the Wild West when I was a girl. There was a lot of moonshine making and most of our neighbors made whiskey. Two of them went to the pen for a year and a day."

Her marriage was arranged. She was not allowed to have horses, cows, dogs, or cats. "He sold my mare and colt for $35. He killed my cat. He tried to drown my two-year-old baby boy, I left."

Redman was the last horse she broke. "He never bucked." As Dorcas got older, she says the ground got harder.

There was a young man from out of town who called himself Joe Smiley. He was pleasant and everyone liked him. The whole town was shocked to see his picture in the paper saying he was killed in Ohio. It was the picture of Joe Smiley but the paper said it was Charles "Pretty Boy" Floyd. "Floyd slept in a nearby barn. He would saddle up every morning and ride all day. Papa often ran into Smiley on local trails." Biographer Michael Wallis has documented that Floyd spent some time around Pueblo but his trail would disappear at times.

Dorcas loved to go elk hunting, camp out and ride horses. "I know I don't need a gun anymore but I keep one because of predators. And I am not afraid to use it if I need to. I still have some livestock. I have had coyotes, bears, lynx, mountain lion and town dogs in my yard. Some survived, some did not. If the wolves they have transplanted to this area jump my fence, they will have a problem. Most wild animals are welcome. Wolves are not. After all, they call me Colorado's Outlaw Granny."

Dorcas had her first heart surgery in 1988. Her cholesterol was 157. After surgery she went on the heart diet and her cholesterol went up to 300. "You can imagine what I did with the diet. Before the second surgery in 2002 it was 158."

Dorcas is the personification of a real pioneer with the type of bold courageous spirit that made the West great. She has survived numerous hardships that only made her stronger. At 83, she still lives in the Four Corners area of southern Colorado. "And I'm still living the good life."—*Connie Vigil Platt*

CLOCKWISE FROM ABOVE: Dorcas, Roma and Earn. Their marriage, which was arranged, didn't last. "When he tried to drown my two-year-old baby boy, I left." ■ Old Urado Schoolhouse. Dorcas is second from left. ■ Her father Earl Hall on Snowball.

PHOTOS COURTESY DORCAS LOWERY

WYOMING . SUMMER 2005

Bud Waldron, 92

Two lion toes were in my trap.

There is longevity in his family, Bud Waldron says, "as long as nobody gets shot."

When Bud was born on February 15, 1912, the doctor arrived by horse and buggy at his parents' Colorado ranch. Bud's daughter Connie traces family ranch locations as far back as 1610 and the area of New York's Wall Street.

Bud's parents, A.J. and Maud, inherited the Buena Vista from A.J.'s parents and established a stable of horses. Around 1900, they made summer pasture with grazing rights on 60,000 acres west of the ranch. "Without that range," Bud says, "the ranch would not have been profitable."

PHOTOS COURTESY BUD WALDRON

Bud, left, in a large, dark hat, at 26th Annual National Western Stock Show in Denver where Bud's shorthorn bull won Reserve Grand Champion in 1932.
RIGHT: Bud with Clydette, "the love of my life."

Bud felt he really began to pull his weight with ranch work when he was six. He rode his pony to school. His dad let him drive a team hitched to a wagon to haul feed and added an extension to the sulky rake trip lever so he could rake the mowed hay. Bud trapped coyotes, bobcats, even a mountain lion. "The lion got away but I had two of his toes in my trap."

One winter, Bud helped a crew move 300-pound cakes of ice cut out of Monument Lake to be stored in an icehouse for summer use in the Denver & Rio Grande Railroad refrigerator cars. "The job only lasted a few weeks and I made 25 cents an hour."

His dad always had a market for colts ready to ride. "There were draft colts, riding colts, and colts for calf roping."

Bud's dad was a director of the Monument State Bank when the Depression struck. The directors paid off loans using their own assets, so college for Bud was no longer an option. For the next four years he trained horses. He also trailed a herd of cattle from Monument to Horse Creek, part of the time in a blizzard. "I was able to save all of them, no losses. I broke even on the deal, but no profit."

He worked every day, "maybe I'd be paid a dollar," Bud recalls, "maybe supper. Never asked ahead of time. There was 30 to 35 percent unemployment."

About this time, Bud accepted a blind date and met the love of his life, Clydette. They were married on Christmas Eve 1933. With a hindquarter of beef wrapped in a sheet in the back of the coupe, the couple took off for California where a gas station job awaited Bud.

When World War II began, Clydette volunteered at the Red Cross. Bud applied at Lockheed Aircraft and within months went from general assembler to radio crew to group leader of the Hudson Bomber Unit.

Even before Pearl Harbor was attacked, there was fear for West Coast aircraft factories. Airplanes were assembled to the point that they could be placed on flatbed trucks and hauled at night to Mojave Air Base in the desert. Bud and four other men rode along to make sure nothing happened. The crew then made the assemblies into planes that could be flown to Arizona and completed.

Bud's practical education served him well. If an aluminum fuel line had to be bent without collapsing, he knew to fill it with sand first. He knew how and when to install a Model-T coil to get a spark to ignite the jets. Later, though with no college degree, Bud was given charge of the Aerospace Electrical Society. He was exhibit manager for the group's expo at the Pan Pacific Auditorium in 1962.

When Bud and Clydette retired with their children, Connie and Bruce, to Mariposa, California, they needed yearling calves to keep the pasture trimmed. Bud built a barn and fencing, bought top quality polled Herefords, purchased a bull and built "an excellent herd of registered cattle."

Produce displays at the Mariposa County Fair were meager. "If I had a sufficient number of display benches," Bud told fair manager Tillie Stroming, "I could fill Building B completely with produce exhibits." Bud drove all over the county, encouraging folks to enter in the fair. He took no credit for filling the exhibit hall to overflowing, but says, "Tillie was a real manager of all things and that made it a great fair."

Bud and Clydette gave the showmanship responsibilities for six head of their cattle to a young girl who belonged to FFA. She needed money for school. When the cattle won prize money, the Waldrons gave it to her.

Bud Waldron has a life motto: "Man is simply unable to construct the higher parts of his destiny, and must know this to survive even the simpler challenges that he is expected to meet."—*Carolyn Fox*

CALIFORNIA . WINTER 2000

Clevon & Anola Dixon, 79 & 83

Packed up like sacks of wheat.

Mention Clevon and Anola Dixon in ranching communities in an area that includes far-northern California, southeastern Oregon and northern Nevada, and folks will smile. That's because the Dixons have friends, all types of friends. As Clevon likes to tell, one day a traveling evangelist stopped by their home in Lake City, a small community in northeastern California's remotely scenic Surprise Valley. "I am going to heaven, I know that," he told Clevon. "I can't wait to get there. How about you?" Clevon says he paused before replying, "It don't make a lot of difference. I've got friends in both places."

Clevon's story began ten miles east of Adel, Oregon, on March 4, 1920. His father, Clarence, was working for other ranchers so his mother, Dixie, was alone. "The doctor couldn't get in," tells Clevon, 79, of his birth. "Mom had five babies before me so it was pretty routine."

From the time Clevon was six months old, his mother packed him in one side of her horse's saddlebags, his two-year-old brother Cecil in the other, and rode ten miles to town to shop. "My mother packed us up like sacks of wheat." And before going home, "she'd put the groceries in with us." Clevon's school learning was brief, lasting only five years. "I never plumb got through grammar school," he admits.

Anola, 83, was born October 28, 1915, on a Nevada ranch 60 miles east of Surprise Valley, the daughter of Jess and Olive Hapgood. Her grandmother had arrived in the area in the early 1870s, after traveling in an oxcart and wagons from Texas. The family's property, the Last Chance Ranch, later became the foundation of the Sheldon National Wildlife Refuge.

"I'm going to heaven, I know that. How about you?" the evangelist asked. Clevon replied, "It don't make a lot of difference. I've got friends in both places."

Anola grew up on the family ranch, two miles from the closest neighbors. During the school year they stayed in Cedarville, California, so she and her siblings could attend school. After high school she worked at the Cedarville telephone office for $30 a month. "I was like a boll weevil looking for a hole," recalls Anola. "I didn't like working in the public." While employed there she met Clevon, who was then an IXL Ranch buckaroo. When they decided to get married in 1942, Anola, then 27, worried about her parents' reaction, "so I left a note and told my folks I'd run off to get married."

PHOTOS COURTESY DIXON FAMILY

Clevon rides bareback at the Lake County Roundup in 1942. ▪ Clevon and Anola enjoy Lake City, California, in the 1990s.

During their early married years they lived on the IXL, between Adel, Oregon, and Denio, Nevada, far from neighbors and the usual conveniences. "We were out 50 miles from nowhere with no car and he was out there breaking horses," remembers Anola, who does not have fond memories of those early years. "I was scared to death of things. I just did it because I had to."

In 1946 they moved to the MC Ranch, where he buckarooed and she worked as the ranch's bookkeeper, and later at the Adel Store. They moved to various ranches, but always returned to the MC, where Clevon eventually worked for 24 years. Clevon was cowboss from 1957 to 1966.

He recalls cattle drives that lasted seven to eleven days while trailing 5,000 cows from Adel to Summer Lake. He tells of standing guard on a herd of cattle in 30 degrees-below-zero weather. But he's proudest of a four-day period when he and other MC buckaroos branded 109, 551, 772 and 295 calves on consecutive days. "If you had 'em in one bunch, you'd try to brand them all," he explains. "To me it was a good experience to work different places. I wanted the kind of jobs so when I quit I could give 'em fifteen minutes' notice."

Lake City has been the Dixons' place since 1966. Clevon has worked as a farrier and for other ranches. For years he broke and trained horses. Anola annually cans up to 500 jars of garden-grown fruits and vegetables. Various illnesses and surgeries have slowed them down, but have not impeded their independence. "That's one advantage of living in the country," smiles Anola. "You can watch the birds if you don't like the people."—*Lee Juillerat*

Update, July 2010
Clevon, 90, Anola, 94

Anola has just recently given up gardening, but still keeps a spotless home and does the laundry. Clevon has the artisan's spirit in figurines he carves from a pine tree on their property. He designed and built a rocking chair that features a shelf for his slippers and shoes, and he still works with leather, including a miniature hackamore and a pair of moccasins that Anola wears.

Five years ago in 2005, Clevon was inducted into the Buckaroo Hall of Fame in Winnemucca, Nevada, held every September, and he has a plaque on his desk along with many other mementos.

Clevon has so many memories of ranches, horses, cattle and cowboys that it would take another lifetime to record them all. He says: "I never finished grammar school. I always said the MC was my high-school education, the Alvord was my college education, and the White Horse was my stretch in reform school. I left the MC four times just to improve my ignorance. The MC was really a good place to work."

When asked if she would cook for the buckaroos at the big outfits while Clevon was cowboss, Anola says she would start getting nervous when one of the cooks would start drinking because she knew Clevon would fire him and she would have to fill in. But she has always been the other half of his life and has pitched in with many jobs.

Now their days are filled with wonderful memories and plenty of visitors to enjoy them with. In a single week, Anola had seven different visitors in seven days. They certainly have earned the right to retire in a cozy spot on their property overlooking the Warner Valley.

—*Linda Dufurrena*

PHOTOS © LINDA DUFURRENA

ABOVE: Clevon and Anola in July 2010, ages 90 and 94.
LEFT: Clevon shows cowboy he carved out of pine from their property.

If life was sometimes hard as the frontier was closing, it could also be good in forming the kind of memories lasting into generations, from a simple lunch in the grass of a remote cowcamp, to an encounter with a sharp-eyed varmint hunter. You still needed to wash your hair and maybe swap some gossip, and come July 4th, there would be some dudes even now who would be impressed by a concert staged in the sagebrush.

ABOVE: R. Marquis photographed three women combing their hair and washing while camping in Wyoming, ca. early 1900s.
AT TOP: R.W. Heck photographed the Pete French crew at the chuck wagon, early 1900s. Charles (Chuck) Goodnight fitted out an army wagon to become the cook wagon/larder for his crews on the Goodnight-Loving Cattle Trail in the 1860s.

CLOCKWISE FROM RIGHT: Photographer McMullen sets up his studio in a tent, ca. 1900. ▪ Coyote Jack, a noted trapper of Harney County, Oregon. ▪ R.W. Heck photo of "Sagebrush Symphony," Burns, Oregon, 1915. ▪ Dressed for a lawn party, this Oregon woman proudly shows the rodent she's just shot. R.W. Heck photo, Burns, Oregon, ca. 1910.

Dorothy Epps, 84

No fence could hold my bull.

A tiny speck with a rooster tail of dust comes speeding across the plain. Drawing near, it takes form as an ATV ridden by a person wrapped in layers of work clothing, wearing a flat-brimmed Australian cattleman's hat and 1950s-era winged sunglasses. Dismounting, the person shucks gloves, opens the gate, sticks out a work-hardened, flinty hand, and says, "Howdy and welcome, I'm Dorothy Epps." At age 84, she's still in the "saddle" and riding hard.

PHOTOS COURTESY DOROTHY EPPS

FROM TOP: Dorothy at sixteen, riding her pet bull, ca. 1929. ▪ Dorothy and mother, Mary Current Brill, attended by hungry lamb, milking in 1918. ▪ Today, still looking good.

It's 35 miles of lonesome blacktop from Dorothy's mailbox to the nearest village, Capitan, New Mexico. It's a few miles more of rough track from the mailbox to her secluded ranch house snuggled in the foothills of the Capitan Mountains. Dorothy commutes to the mailbox by ATV and drives her pickup truck to town only if she absolutely has to. She has been living in this isolated corner of the West since 1913. Her father, Nicholas Brill, homesteaded the land in 1909 after the gold mines in White Oaks, New Mexico, played out.

"My daddy was German," Dorothy says. "He was living in El Paso, Texas, when the White Oaks strike occurred. He walked from El Paso to the mines in the late 1800s. He ran goats for the Kessler family near Carrizozo until he settled here. My momma, Mary Current, was English and from Breckenridge, Texas. Her daddy had a ranch in the Patos Mountains, a day's buggy ride away."

Dorothy's first memory of growing up on the Brill Ranch was riding behind her father on a horse. "In the 1920s, the nearest railhead was in Capitan. My dad and I drove our cattle cross-county to get there. It took four days and three nights on the trail. It was hard work, but worth it just to have a chance to go to town. Got mighty lonely on the ranch. It was a long way to anywhere. When Dad went to town for supplies he drove the wagon and team to Roswell. Took him a week to make the trip."

The young ranch lass rode a paint burro miles to school. She remembers the schoolteacher, Warren Rockwell. "The school's name was Bethel, but everybody took to calling it Hog Wallow because during parties the cowboys would git loop-legged and wallow around on the ground. Had better parties up in the Capitans at a place called Pine Lodge. Folks would ride and drive teams 50 or 60 miles for a party. Took so long to git there we'd just dance all night."

Recreation was pretty much self-made on the Brill Ranch. Dorothy had a gentle bull to ride. "Had one broke to a saddle and a bridle; he was tame to ride but there wouldn't be a fence made that would hold him!"

Dorothy's speech is boiled down to bare bones; characteristic of a person too darn busy working to make small talk. There is not a scrap of embroidery on anything that she says, but during the 1950s an event happened on the land adjacent to the Brill Ranch that still receives worldwide attention—the Roswell incident.

"A writer from *Forbes* magazine, I think it was, called the ranch and asked for permission to cross it. He said a flying saucer had crashed on the mountainside. It was the one that crashed on the Arabella-Pine Lodge Road on the mountain behind our ranch. I let him and his girlfriend cross, and they each came back with a tow sack of stuff from the flying saucer. I don't know exactly what happened, but the bags and his girlfriend disappeared. I will say this. I haven't seen one, but I believe in flying saucers."

Dorothy and her 24-year-old granddaughter, Mary Folkner, work the ranch every day, tending the cattle and fences on their ATVs. They work hard and eat a lot of beef and venison. "Keeps me going; it's energy food," Dorothy says. "I'm 84 and it ain't hurt me yet!"

Young Mary is learning ranching at her grandma's side. "Mary is the fourth generation to work this land and the fifth one is coming up fast," the old lady says proudly. "If the environmentalists don't put us out of business, we'll be here for many more generations."

—*J. Zane Walley*

NEVADA . FALL 2003

Frederick 'Fritzie' Buckingham, 80

A short, wild ride.

Watching the Bar X cattle wend their way through the sagebrush, Frederick "Fritzie" Buckingham stands ready to open the gates. He and ten border collie/blue heeler-mix dogs wait for his son Bob and two ranch hands to bring the herd down from summer range.

Paradise Valley is fed by snowmelt, Little Humboldt River and several bold streams. Fritzie's great-grandfather Charles Kemler built the first house in 1865. He had emigrated from Germany and soon lost an arm in a mine blast in California. Undaunted, he went on to drive a jerkline team, hauling wagonloads of supplies to the mines.

Conflict with Indians resulted in the building of Camp Winfield Scott nearby in 1866, and the burgeoning town was named Scottsdale, later changed to Paradise Valley. Lying 40 miles northeast of Winnemucca in Nevada's Humboldt County, the town grew in importance as a mining supply center and stagecoach stop. Charles Kemler built a flour mill in Winnemucca and a store in Paradise Valley.

In 1916, Fritzie's grandmother, Anna Kemler Buckingham, bought a black seven-passenger King V8 automobile in Sacramento. Her son Fritz drove the new car home to Paradise Valley and commented that he didn't see another car on the road. Seven years later, he took his wife back to her mother's home in Sacramento for the birth of Fritzie, as his father dubbed him.

"About half of these dogs work and the other half catch mice, but they would all rather just ride in the pickup with me."

In Paradise Valley, the family kept a flock of sheep and tiny Fritzie began his riding career with a short wild ride on the back of a wether. "My chores included milking cows, feeding chickens and raking hay, but I much preferred working with the horses. My first horse was a bay mustang colt."

Fritzie ranched until 1944 when the U.S. Army had other plans. "After boot camp at Camp Roberts in Paso Robles, California, I served two years in the Pacific during World War II. After the war, I returned to Paradise Valley and acquired the 1,000-acre Fort Scott Ranch on Cottonwood Creek." In 1970, a brief illness forced him to sell the ranch and move his herd to Winnemucca.

He returned to Paradise Valley in 1976 and purchased the Bar X Ranch, forming a partnership with his son, Bob. Bar X cattle run on the Granite Peak Forest allotment during the summer months. Ranching in the mountains can spell trouble when snow traps steers at higher elevations. "A few years ago, some of the Bar X cattle faced starvation until they were spotted by helicopter and a trail was broken out by ranchers on snowshoes and snowmobiles."

Wintered on the ranch, the cattle are fed alfalfa, wheat and grass hay grown on the Bar X and a farm purchased in 1993.

Years ago, cattle buyers came to the ranches and offered a price; take it or leave it. To get a feel for the market, cattlemen from Paradise Valley attended stock auctions at Fort McDermitt Indian Reservation on the Oregon border. Once sold, a three-day drive to the stockyards in Winnemucca put the cattle at the railroad for shipping. Lately, Bob and Fritzie have begun selling feeder stock on video.

"Ranching's always been difficult, but I wouldn't have wanted to do anything else. Life is the calendar; I look forward to longer days, then seeing the grass green up."

—*Katharine Jensen*

© KATHARINE JENSEN

PHOTO COURTESY AMERICAN FOLKLIFE CENTER

PHOTO COURTESY FRITZIE BUCKINGHAM

CLOCKWISE FROM TOP: Fritzie and a few of his multiple hounds. ▪ Fritzie shows off his blue-ribbon bull Mark G. Domino II in 1941. ▪ Fritzie's dad with Paiute Tommy Abel around 1912.

Bob & Mary Bowman, 88 & 89

The perfect setting.

Modern ways of doing things hadn't quite caught up with Sonoita, Arizona, when Bob and Mary Bowman arrived from California in 1955 looking for good ranch property to purchase. The couple saw a ranch they liked but weren't able to locate the owner before their return flight, so Bob says, "We

PHOTOS COURTESY BOB AND MARY BOWMAN

ABOVE: Mary and Bob Bowman, Backward B Spear Ranch in Box Canyon, December 2006.
RIGHT: Anthony Quinn (left), star of "Last Train From Gun Hill," with Bob and Mary during filming at the neighboring Empire Ranch in 1959. Once the roundup crew left, it was up to Bob to brand and doctor the stragglers on his own.

decided to send a letter to the closest Chamber of Commerce, located about 25 miles west in Nogales."

Although they never received a reply to this optimistically addressed missive, the Bowmans soon returned and with the help of a realtor, found a perfect gem of a ranch nestled in Box Canyon at the foothills of the majestic Santa Rita Mountains. They dubbed it the Backward B Spear, and it has been the headquarters for their cattle ranching operations and renowned barbecues ever since.

Mary says: "When we moved in we had a small TV set and the first night, when the Tucson newscast came on, we couldn't believe it. The weatherwoman said, 'If Bob and Mary Bowman are listening tonight, please get in touch with the Schorrs. They are anxious to meet their new neighbors.'" That warm welcome set the tone for the Bowmans' long love affair with the land and the people of the local area.

The rolling grasslands afforded not only scenic views but also the perfect setting for their Hereford cow/calf operation. "When it was time to gather," Bob says, "the whole community got involved, with ranchers and crews traveling round-robin for the brandings. More often than not the last stop of the day would be the Backward B Spear, where I always had ribs (make that beef ribs, please) sizzling on the grill." Even today, when the menu occasionally calls for that other meat, Bob always throws some beef ribs on the back of the grill. "No day is complete without a good dose of red meat!"

Although now retired from cattle ranching, both Bob and Mary continue their enthusiastic support of the community. They have no children of their own, but are godparents many times over and loyal supporters of 4-H. Every year at the county fair Bob and Mary can be counted on to buy a steer, a lamb or a pig and donate it back to raise more funds for programs to keep youngsters involved in ranching and farming.

"We feel very frustrated that extreme environmental and wildlife-protection activists seem to have an agenda to put ranchers out of business," Bob explains, "because ranchers have been the true custodians of our land and an important part of our economy for generations."

Mary has served on the school board and volunteered at the hospital in Tucson. Bob has donated hours of service to the fairgrounds association, including a five-year stint as president. A self-taught historian, in 1998 Bob came up with an idea to preserve some of the local history at an archives center to be located at the fairgrounds. "There were no personal accounts of the homesteaders and families who first settled this community, and I was afraid that if we didn't get it down on paper soon, it would all be lost."

He collected photos and documents relating to the beginnings of the Fair & Rodeo Association, along with histories and memorabilia of the early settlers, and developed a room to display them. The impressive collection was officially dedicated as the Bowman Archives Center in 2003.

Bob and Mary Bowman have truly had a long love affair with the land and the people of Sonoita. As Mary says so well: "All my life, this is what I wanted to do. I am very grateful."—*Betty Barr*

OKLAHOMA . SUMMER 1999

Mark Freeman, 79

A few cows, a few sows, a few hundred dollars and a dream.

Mark Freeman is silent as he rambles his feed truck along a line of cows eagerly eating up the cake he's just strung out. "We're short," he announces at the far end, wheeling the truck around so he can scan the Osage hills unfolding in all directions. This is his country—a considerable chunk of native range rolling north of Pawhuska, Oklahoma, on up to the Kansas line. This is where Mark's heart and soul live, a place he's been traveling toward ever since he was a kid.

Born in Ponca City, Oklahoma, in 1920 of Osage and Kaw heritage, Mark grew up during the Great Depression—hardscrabble times when self-reliance was more necessity than option. As a boy in the 1930s, he had three milk cows, selling cream and providing milk for his family. He also sold chickens for 25 cents a pound live weight, with another dime for cleaning and delivery. By the time he was out of high school, he had a few cows, a few sows, a few hundred dollars and a dream. "I always wanted a hundred cows and the ground they stood on," he says. "Back in those days a man could make a life out of a hundred cows."

World War II temporarily sidetracked Mark when he left Ponca City and entered the Marine Corps to become a flight navigator and later a pilot. While on leave during the war, he bought his first place—400 acres near home—and when the war ended, he started back down the road toward becoming a rancher.

The track wasn't smooth though, and Mark did what he had to do to keep the dream going. He didn't like milking cows, but in the 1950s, due to drought and low cattle prices, milking 100 head of Holsteins kept his family fed and his goals on target.

PHOTOS © MARK PARKER

AT TOP: Mark Freeman says: "People say it's just too damn expensive for a young fella to get started in ranching or farming. Well, they were wrong then and they're wrong now." But he admits, "You might have to have an outside job or lease land or milk cows or haul hay." BOTTOM: Mark on his nine-year-old paint.

Starting from scratch is never easy, and for all the changes in the world of agriculture in the past half-century, Mark believes today's young food producers face the same challenge.

"It's impossible for a young person to get started in agriculture—that's something I've heard all my life. The reasons change, but it's always been the same. People say it's just too damn expensive for a young fella to get started in ranching or farming. Well, they were wrong then and they're wrong now. It can be done."

Each generation has different problems to face. "In the 1930s, the problem was no credit, no money and no jobs. Today there's a different set of problems, but it adds up to the same thing. Land's too high but you've got to have a home base to work from, land that can't be taken away from you."

Mark often says never say never, no such thing as a free lunch. "They're all clichés, but if you live long enough you find out just how true they are," he says. "You've got to put away for those bad times during the good. Now I know it's not really that simple. Things get complicated sometimes, but that's got to be what you strive for. In the cattle business, I've always tried to be in a position to buy some cattle when nobody else wanted to buy and to sell some cattle when everybody else wanted to buy."

With a wink, Mark adds, "Luck is an important part of success, but once in a while you can make your own luck. You've just got to be prepared to take advantage of situations when they come up."

At the ranch headquarters, Mark saddles up a good-looking paint gelding and explains that he bought himself a four-year-old to ride back when he was a mere 61. He kind of figured that horse would be the last one he'd ever have to buy, but it didn't work out that way. His new paint is now nine and Mark allows that he may need a replacement someday.—*Mark Parker*

Surely the sun must shine longer on Nebraska. From dawn along the crease of the Platte until it seems to fall away across the western curvature of earth, it seems never to snare a shadow. A long day's work in summer might find a hungry man scuffing home in the quiet light of a stunning universe with a bright moon over his shoulder just as lost.

ONE-ROOM SCHOOLHOUSE, UNUSED, IN THE SAND HILLS OF NEBRASKA.
PHOTO © LARRY ANGIER

Florence A. (Sandoz) Fisher, 84

Almost killed by the rake teeth.

"I started riding horses when I was two. I was horse crazy and rode all the time. I had a little sorrel horse called Rex that I rode to school, and I taught him all kinds of tricks," says Sandhills cowgirl Florence Fisher. "When I graduated from high school, my parents gave me the choice of a watch or a horse for a present. I chose the horse—a palomino mare named Polly."

Florence was born in Hay Springs, Nebraska, in 1922, the youngest of five children to Swiss immigrants, Felix and Esther Sandoz. Cousin "Old Jules" Sandoz became famous through the literary work of his daughter, Mari.

"We raised cattle, and my dad hunted coyotes to pay his land taxes during the 1930s," she says. "If you had a good horse and good hounds, you could sometimes get three coyotes in a day." Their ranch bordered the Cravath ranch, and for fourteen years Florence's parents partnered with Minnie Cravath in the cattle business. When Minnie passed away in 1938, she willed $1,000 to Florence. "I guess I was like the kid she never had. I bought ten purebred Hereford heifer calves with that money." In 1939, she registered her own brand—the Lazy SS. "Then I got in the horse business with a stud and a couple mares."

In 1940, Florence married handsome local cowboy Buford Fisher. He was breaking horses at the Fort Robinson remount station for $35 a month. Their daughter Karen and son Gary were born before Buford was drafted into the Navy. He served in the South Pacific, testing munitions during World War II.

Florence could do almost anything on the ranch. "During the summer of 1946, our hired man quit. Buford was mowing hay with a tractor, and in the absence of a hired man, I was raking hay with a team of roan mares. We stopped to visit for a few minutes and when he started up, he gave the tractor the choke so it wouldn't die. It made a loud pop, and my mares started to run.

"I was several months pregnant and knew I couldn't stay with them, so I slipped down and put my arm around the seat. I knew if I let go, the rake teeth would kill me. I pulled one line and got the mares to run in a circle. When they came by Buford, he ran out and grabbed them. The rake had been dumping and hitting me in the back each time. Both mother and baby were fine. "My dad's sister, Jennie, died that way. A team ran away with her, and every time the rake teeth fell, they pierced her, and it killed her."

—Echo (Fisher) Renner

PHOTOS COURTESY FLORENCE FISHER

CLOCKWISE FROM LEFT: Florence and Buford. He was cowboying for $35 a month. ▪ This is Florence in 1939. ▪ Training Rex to sit. ▪ Hound Curley is guarding Florence with a coyote they caught on the way to school.

NORTH DAKOTA . FALL 1996

Harold Lowman, 84

Picking potatoes, riding freights.

PHOTOS COURTESY LOWMAN FAMILY

Ann and Harold meet three-month-old great-granddaughter Samantha in 1995.

During the hard times of the Great Depression, folks living out on the land didn't have much. But they shared what they had and as long as there was meat on the table, a meal could be built around it. This philosophy has carried Harold Lowman through 84 years of cowboying around the western states.

Born in the mining town of Ulysses, Idaho, in January 1912, Harold was only a few days old when a snowslide buried the cabin. When his miner father Charles returned home, he had to get help to dig his wife Ida Marie and children out. The family moved around a lot, with Harold's dad working in the mines or on ranches. It was a lonely life for his young wife Ida and it wasn't too many years until she returned to her parents in Morrill, Nebraska.

The young lad spent several years with his dad in Idaho, Washington and Nevada. At six, he spent the "winter of the flu" boarding with a Spokane, Washington, family as his dad worked nearby. Many died that winter and the family he was staying with all took sick. Harold muses, "Someone sure had their arms around a lonely little boy so far from home."

While still a small boy, he went with his dad and a herd of sheep up into the Seven Devils Mountains along Idaho's Snake River. They camped out all summer until they brought the band back down in the fall. They used to hang a slab of bacon in a tree alongside their tent. During one night, a bear stood up on its hind legs and got the bacon off its hook, only a couple of feet from where Harold lay sleeping in his soogan. Next morning they tracked the bear up a canyon and shot it.

Harold got a little classroom schooling back in Nebraska when he stayed with his mother, but at fourteen he quit school and he and his older brother struck out on their own. They picked potatoes, and rode the freight trains; these were hungry times.

At nineteen, during the Great Depression, Harold worked on a big sheep outfit in Nevada. Wages were $90 per month. He even had a few hundred dollars in the bank. But as the economy slipped and the boss dropped their winter pay to $40 a month, Harold quit.

Harold hunted by horseback with his oldest son Jim, and bagged this buck on Wanagan Creek in 1950.

Meanwhile, his brother had thrown in with a young cowboy to run wild horses in the Dakota Badlands. Cheap land could be bought in North Dakota because the county had repossessed many homesteads for back taxes. Land was selling for 50 cents an acre. His brother wired Harold for money to buy some.

Harold followed the cowboys to North Dakota and as he stepped off the train in Sentinel Butte in the dead of winter, 1931, he found a bleak and desolate world. Drought and overstocking had taken a toll on the range and he only stayed because he was now a property owner. He grins, "I found a man with a Maxwell car and gave him four silver dollars to take me out to where my brother and two other young fellers were shacked up in an old abandoned homestead." Those hungry cowboys were glad to see him arrive with a few groceries.

As the Depression worsened, his brother and friends moved on. Jobs were hard to find, Harold says, "so they rode the grub line." A cowboy would ride into a ranch looking for a free meal. Usually folks were glad to have someone to visit with and catch up on the news, as there were no phones or newspapers in the country at that time. If the rancher needed a little help, the cowboy stayed on for a few days and worked—for room and board. Then it was saddle up and drift to the next place.

During these times, nobody had any money, so they made their own entertainment with rodeos, barn dances, card parties and basket socials. At a Fourth of July dance, Harold met the girl who would become his bride. "If somebody had a car and some gas, you went in style," he recalls. "But many times you rode long miles horseback to dance all night then rode home again." Those high-backed saddles allowed them to doze off; the horse knew the way home.

The prolonged drought of the '30s forced many people to give up, pull up stakes, and move westward; others returned to their families in the East.

When the rains finally came, the country healed. Harold had managed to hang on to his property and kept adding to it. He and Ann, his wife of 55 years, still live on the home place. Their youngest son and his family live nearby and operate the ranch today. "Now we have electricity, phone and mail that comes every day," Harold says with a smile. "Shucks, we live like town folks!"—*Jim Lowman*

OREGON . SPRING 1999

Ray Taylor, 81

Damned near starved to death selling Studebakers.

Life has never been easy for Ray Taylor. But even if they weren't always good times, at least they were his times.

Home was a two-story house outside of a tiny hamlet. It had fifteen-inch-thick sandstone walls and was built along Willow Creek, where his family raised cattle, chickens, alfalfa, hogs, and vegetables in their garden. "That's God's country," says Ray. "They can raise anything. They got all kinds of water. I fed the hogs watermelon and cantaloupes. Everybody raised something they didn't want or couldn't use and you fed it to the hogs."

Wild pheasants were a common meal. When he and other family members harvested fields with mowing machines, slow-flying pheasants would often get clipped by the whirling blades. Those with broken legs ended up on dinner plates. "Them was the good ol' days!" Fun times, but also hard times.

Once Brogan, Oregon, had a railroad, hotel, acres of apples and fruit orchards, an apple-packing shed and a rosy future. But a drought that started in the 1920s dried out the orchards, causing economic chaos. Ray's family suffered financially and emotionally during the Great Depression. In 1930, when he was just thirteen, his father George committed suicide. George had deposited the family earnings in a bank only a day before it crashed and went out of business. It was two weeks before Christmas.

The second of four children and the only boy, Ray was born in the family home and raised wild and free. He rode horseback from the time he was able to sit behind his father. "During the summer, when we weren't doing anything, we'd get out and chase them damn horses. We could never catch 'em. Just as soon as you showed up, they could smell you and they were gone."

Ray tells of threshing bees, where neighbors helped each other with harvests, and of Fourth of July gatherings at his family's home, where his mother made homemade ice cream. "People'd come to our house and Dad would say, 'Put your horse in the back and give him some hay and stay all night.' Never worried 'bout people doing any harm."

PHOTOS COURTESY RAY TAYLOR

ABOVE: Ray's family in 1914, from left: Dad holding Dorothy, Mother, Daisy Irvin, John Irvin, Grandpa Burdick. ▪ Ray enjoyed the bootleg days. "Things was wide open."

Ray lived eighteen years in Brogan, leaving while still in high school for the eastern Oregon town of Baker, where he worked for the Forest Service and Civilian Conservation Corps. Then he worked in Sacramento before enlisting in the Air Force in 1940. He shipped out to Australia, New Guinea and the Philippines and, after the war, sold Studebakers in Fresno. "Damned near starved to death." In 1947 he moved to Klamath Falls, Oregon, and hasn't moved since.

"I got married, and I got stuck," he explains with a grin. Ray and his wife Lorraine were married in 1949. After Lorraine's death in 1987, he married Betty.

Ray worked at various mills, including the Big Lakes Lumber Mill, Weyerhaeuser and Jeld-Wen, until he retired in 1982. "I was never out of a job very long. I lucked out. We had five kids. You have to keep your nose to the grindstone. It was steady work and pretty good pay."

During the worst of times, he and his family largely lived off the land—milk from cows, fruits and vegetables from the garden, and meat from pigs, chickens and cattle. "I knew the value of a buck," Ray says. The family earned money for food staples like flour and yeast by selling cream to local dairies. "We had what we grew and raised. I felt sorry for the people in town. They had to stand in soup lines. We was lucky."

—*Lee Juillerat*

MONTANA . SPRING 2006

Peg Allen, 85

Biting and chewing that little rascal into the world.

Peg Allen was a blonde 23-year-old city slicker when she convinced her husband that they should leave Chicago and move to Montana to become cattle ranchers. "We had no idea what we were doing, but it sounded like fun," says the spry 85-year-old, "and it sure was!"

That first ranch was near Yellowstone National Park, ten miles up a rough dirt road in Paradise Valley. It was there that she was forced to come up with the list that has lasted 55 years.

"It was during a bad snowstorm," she says. "The road crew finally reached our place, but told me they wouldn't be able to come back for at least two weeks, so I'd better dash to town and get supplies while I had time. I sat right down and tried to figure what supplies were really necessary for the next month. I made a long list. I kept it, and it still works. Numbers one and two on that list were easy. I figure if you have enough toilet paper and a wee drop of booze you can face anything."

Peg takes a rest on one of her tame bulls. She's wearing a pistol on her hip. "It's a .357 Magnum and I never go into the mountains without it."

Peg is a widow now—her hair has turned white and her two children are adults—but she still operates a small ranch on the outskirts of Livingston. She has lived through successful breast-cancer surgery, diabetes, and full hip replacement—but she was back in the saddle within four months.

She remembers the night she heard a cow bellowing in the barn. "I jumped up, pulled on my boots, and ran. I found she had delivered her baby, but it was still in the sac on the floor under her. I could see the baby moving a little, but knew I didn't have much time to get it out. I tried to tear the sac open, but it was too tough. I couldn't find a knife or scissors, so I did the only thing I could—used my teeth. I bit and ripped and chewed that little rascal into the world. The mother came over and licked her baby—and then turned and licked me."

On many other occasions over the years she helped cows become mothers by giving their "dead" calves dedicated help. One night she entered the barn to check on a cow due to deliver, and discovered that the calf's leg and head were sticking out already. The head was all purple and there was no movement to the protruding tongue.

"I ran back to the house and grabbed Arch. I told him we had to get the dead calf out before it killed the mother too."

Arch entertained the mother while Peg pushed the baby all the way back in, just as the mother had another contraction so strong she thought her arm would fall off. She got the leg in proper position, attached a rope and pulled the dead baby out. "Too bad, I said to Arch as we looked down at the beautiful lifeless little bull. Then Arch suddenly said, 'Hey. He winked at you!' So we went to work. Arch began pushing up and down on the bull's chest while I alternated between giving it mouth-to-mouth resuscitation and tickling its nose with hay. Suddenly there was an explosive sneeze that brought the little guy hopping right into life."

Peg was at a cattle auction once where she was asked if her bulls were "lady broke."

"I had never heard that term before, and began asking questions. I learned that some bulls have a frightened reaction to women. They can get mean and testy just like a stallion. I also learned that many ranchers won't buy a bull that hasn't been lady broke.

"Up until then I pretty much avoided bulls, figuring they were men's work. But I set out to prove to our bulls that I was not a threat. I approached cautiously until they were used to having me around. Then I'd pet them, comb them, give them special goodies to eat, and turned them into pals."

Peg's work with cattle earned her the nickname The Bull Baroness, with a roomful of blue ribbons and trophies as she became one of the West's top experts on cattle breeding. "I was the first woman to lead a bull into the big winter fair ring in Billings—where I always got several hundred dollars above normal because they were lady broke."

She laughs and adds, "We got to live in a valley which God made when he was having a really good day, and to enjoy all the marvelous seasons we have here. Winter can be tough now and then, but I just figure it is the price of the pearl. And I still have my list."

—*Bill Kiley*

Nevada has three substantial rivers that flow down from the mountains and simply disappear in the Great Basin, never reaching the sea. This was once a vast inland ocean that scientists believe may still exist in some form of a deep aquifer, leaving the lands above surprisingly fertile in valleys well suited for livestock and farms that, with time, do make the high desert bloom.

MOONSET OVER BUFF PEAK, NORTH JACKSON MOUNTAINS. PHOTO © LINDA DUFURRENA

Leota Pfingsten, 70ish

Ranching schoolmarm, almost raised by a jack.

PHOTOS COURTESY PFINGSTEN FAMILY

TOP, left to right: Leota at age twelve, sister Freddie Lee and mother Maggie Lou at the Sweetwater Ranch in 1928. Leota says, "At times we got so hot, tired and thirsty, I would have swapped the whole shebang for one cold Coca-Cola." BOTTOM: Leota and Fred pose with their Studebaker Freight Wagon.

When first meeting Leota Bradford Pfingsten, it's hard to believe this educated, eloquent and impeccable lady has a pioneer ranching history stretching back more than 70 years. Yet Leota has worked stock in the blistering heat of the sun-blasted San Andres Mountains and in the deep winter snows on the White Mountains.

Leota's parents, Maggie Lou and Frederick Bradford, began ranching Angora goats around Salinas Peak in the San Andres Mountains of New Mexico in 1915, 25 miles south of what is now known as the Trinity site. Maggie and the children lived in Alamogordo, working at the Sweetwater Ranch headquarters during school vacations and holidays. Leota loved those days. "We rode burros, and had a mammoth jack, Old Johnny. He was like a family member. I was almost raised by him!"

She remembers a time they were riding across a stretch of pan rock on Salinas Mountain when he froze, stopping dead in his tracks. "I yelled and kicked, but he wouldn't move an inch. Then I noticed a rattlesnake slithering between his legs. He wouldn't budge until it was long gone."

The family ran over 3,000 head of goats, keeping them in flocks of about 500 and employing one herder for each group. "Our herders lived so isolated, we'd have to pack supplies to them by burro," Leota recalls. "It was a hard life for them, especially the weather. During one drought, a *bracero* was cutting hearts out of sotol [a yucca-like plant] for the goats to eat. Lightning struck him, blowing his shoes to pieces, and burning his hip where the canteen was hanging. Remarkably he lived and fully recovered."

Desert storms were sudden devastation. Steep, arid canyons became raging torrents in minutes, drowning livestock caught in flash floods. "During one blow, we lost 600 head," Leota recalls. "But most of the time it was bone dry."

Water was scarce in the mountains of the Chihuahua Desert, so rare that Spanish explorers had named the valley west of the ranch *Jornada del Muerto*—Journey of Death. Leota recalls how every drop of water was prized. "We piped water from springs high on Salinas Peak to a big stock tank at Sweetwater. Once Momma's car rolled down the hill, knocked a hole in the side, and started a leak. We tried everything to stop the trickle, and finally plugged it with goat manure. My daddy just couldn't stand to see that water get away."

The ranch lass from Alamogordo attended college at Las Cruces in the 1930s. True to her rural roots, she dated and married fellow student, cowboy/rancher Fred Pfingsten from Capitan. Leota says, "After the wedding, we lived on a ranch in the Rio Bonito Valley—ran cattle in the high country of the Sacramento Mountains for the summer, and wintered them on lowland grassy bottoms leased from the railroad."

Leota began her teaching career while on the Rio Bonito ranch. "In 1940, my husband and I had been to a Saturday roping in Alamogordo. When we came home I found a note on the gate asking me to teach at Hondo School starting on Monday. I owned only one dress, my wedding dress, so I washed and ironed it to teach in, until I could make it to town and buy more clothes."

Leota taught at Hondo for two years, until the railroad planted their grazing lease in trees. "We could no longer graze livestock on the Rio Bonito. Had to move to Nogal Mesa in the mountains, so we could care for the cattle."

Winters often lasted from September until Easter. "We'd get snowed in for long stretches, couldn't travel for the deep snow," Leota recalls with a shiver. "We ate beef, a lot of it, to keep us warm through those winters. As a matter of fact, we still do."

Leota retired from teaching in 1978. She and Fred are still ranching cattle on ten sections of rough country in the watersheds of the White and Capitan mountains. During long winter nights, she regularly plies chisel and knife, carving her western legacy into native woods.

Taking a coffee break from the carving bench, Leota smiles with clear blue eyes when thinking of her past. "I taught second grade, and loved to see children blossoming, awakening, day by day. I used music to reach them. If they didn't like math or spelling, I'd put it to music. Never did meet a child I couldn't reach with music."

She says she has absolutely enjoyed her life, as diverse as it's been. She's been happy everywhere she's lived, but she adds, "Of all I've done, I loved teaching the most."—*J. Zane Walley*

Jim W. Kinney, 88

Still kickin'.

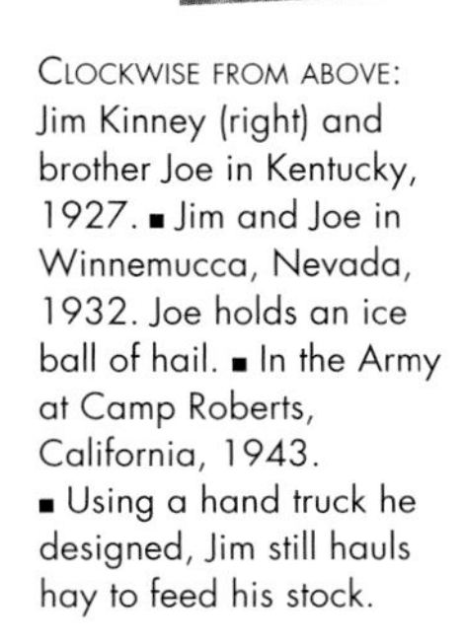

CLOCKWISE FROM ABOVE: Jim Kinney (right) and brother Joe in Kentucky, 1927. ■ Jim and Joe in Winnemucca, Nevada, 1932. Joe holds an ice ball of hail. ■ In the Army at Camp Roberts, California, 1943. ■ Using a hand truck he designed, Jim still hauls hay to feed his stock.

PHOTOS COURTESY KINNEY FAMILY

Ask Jim Kinney how he's doing and he'll reply, "Still kickin'!" And he's fortunate that still kickin' applies even after breaking his back at his Winnemucca, Nevada, ranch two years ago. Standing on the back of his truck to reach a 120-pound bale atop his haystack, Jim was knocked to the ground when it toppled, fracturing three vertebrae. With nobody in shouting range, Jim crawled over 100 yards to his home to phone for help. Lifelong friend Leland York drove him to the hospital and cared for Jim's cattle while he was incapacitated.

Despite surgery, 88-year-old Jim suffers persistent pain. "The only time my back doesn't hurt is when I'm lyin' flat in bed," he says. Forced to sell most of his cattle, Jim still cares for a tiny herd of five cows, a bull and their calves. "Old age and pain have slowed me down, but those cows are the reason I get up each day!"

Jim started life on a farm belonging to his parents, George and Cleo Kinney, in Little Cypress, Kentucky. His father didn't stick with farming; instead, he managed Railroad Express Agency offices in small towns where Jim and his brother Joe enjoyed the outdoors. Finally, the family settled in Winnemucca when Jim was fourteen and Joe was ten. Jim's love of the outdoors inspired his desire to ranch.

After graduating from Humboldt County High School in 1936, Jim worked as a clerk in the Winnemucca Post Office and bought land to start ranching. World War II interrupted his plans. Jim, Joe and 27 other Winnemucca residents were inducted into the Army on the same day in 1942. Setting aside his plans, Jim sold his property and spent nearly four years in the military. He was stationed in both the Pacific and European theaters. In the 26th Infantry Division, D Company of the 101st Regiment, Jim served under Gen. George S. Patton, and fought in the Battle of the Bulge.

"We landed on Omaha Beach right after D-Day. The fires were still burning and the bodies were still there. From then on, I served on the front lines. For the next year and a half, we almost never missed a day when we weren't shot at!" Looking back on his military career, Jim says, "I wouldn't trade it, but I wouldn't want to do it again!"

"That old mare ran away every time she got a load. I was young then and could keep up with her!"

After the war, Jim returned to Winnemucca and became the youngest postmaster in the country, a position he held until retirement in 1972. The job financed several ranch properties and Jim's cattle venture with up to 200 "tails."

Jim built his home using a borrowed Belgian horse and a slip scraper to dig the basement. "That old mare ran away every time she got a load. I was young then and could keep up with her! We'd dump the load and she'd quit. I'd take her back in the hole and start all over again!"

Once Jim tried raising sheep. "I only kept the sheep for a couple of years. They were all over the place…too hard to corral and always eatin' the neighbors' flowers!" Later he specialized in registered polled-Hereford bulls.

A bachelor with no nearby family to help, Jim found creative ways to continue ranching into his senior years. To haul heavy hay bales, he devised a hand truck with bicycle wheels that won't get stuck in mud or snow. His cattle are also well trained. "They know that a ride in the trailer means a trip to greener pastures," Jim says. "They don't give me any problems when it's time to move; they line up to get onboard."

Jim still drives them to market in Fallon when, as he says, "they make their trip to the greenest pasture of all!"

—Judy Kinney Tidrick

CALIFORNIA . FALL 1993

Pete Gerig, 100

Not dead yet.

Tap. Tap-tap-tap. A few days past his 100th birthday party in late April, Pete Gerig is changing part of a poem he composed for the occasion on his 1923 Underwood typewriter:

"*and this is the message I want you to get, I'm still a kicking and I ain't dead yet*"

He had read his poem to the assembled throng of family and friends on the day of the celebration. Never mind that everyone else is astonished by the agility of his mind, by his walking around aided only by a cane, and by his having written any poem at all. Vivid and colorful though his verses may be, he knows they could stand some improving.

Pete thinks about it as he sits at the small table in the cluttered, tiny office

© JAMES CRANE

that his 95-year-old wife Bulah calls his disaster room. From his window, he can watch the green of spring brighten the sprawling meadows, pasture and sage-covered hills of Big Valley in northeastern California. He can keep an eye on his 55-year-old grandson Peter and his 28-year-old great-grandson Bryan as they go about their chores.

Pete says he has no advice for people who hope to live to a ripe old age. "I wasn't too much of a leader of organizations. I belonged to 'em, but I didn't care about the leadership. I think leadership wears people out faster." He concedes that he was a member of the Lassen County Board of Supervisors for 28 years, he served on the planning commission for more than two decades, and has held at least half a dozen other public-service posts.

Perhaps the hard physical work of ranching was a healthy balance for his sedentary political and public-service jobs. He prides himself on having been the greatest hay stacker of his day, making "nice, square, straight up-and-down stacks." But while that might explain his longevity, what about Pete's sisters—Bertie Mumma, 102, and Ketura Farmer, 97. Gerig family doctor Dan Dahle says its members plainly have extraordinarily hard-wearing genes. Pete's grandson thinks he understands the old man's longevity. "Lots of sex and whiskey," Bryan teases. "That's how Grandpa got to be a hunnerd!"

Bulah Gerig—whom Pete married in 1975 after the death of his first wife, Leona—says it's because her husband is sweet-tempered. "We haven't ever fought. Haven't even had a real good argument in seventeen years," she says, beaming. They attended the same school as children and never lived more than a few miles apart. She was surprised when he proposed, but she never let him back down. "Once he said the words," she laughs, "he was stuck!"

He has spurned opportunities to visit the German part of Switzerland that is the land of his father's people. "Home suits me too well," he explains. He says his family's ranch—partially acquired under the Swamp Act of 1841, in which land was given away to ranchers willing to drain it—has changed little since his boyhood. But Pete is appalled by the economics of ranching today.

"I used to hire men for a dollar or two a day and we worked from six 'til six. Now they pay ten or fifteen dollars a day! Gosh, I don't know how people make it."—*Cheryll Aimee Barron*

ON TURNING A HUNDRED

By Pete Gerig

My hair is white and I am almost blind
The days of my youth are far behind
My neck is stiff, I can't turn my head
Can't hear one-half that is being said
My legs are wobbly, can hardly walk
And it takes a pill to make me talk
My joints are stiff, won't turn in their sockets
And nary a dime do I have in my pocket.
But still do I have a lot of fun
My heart with joy is overrun
I have friends—so kind and sweet
And many more that I'll never meet
So take it from me and don't forget
I'm still a living and I ain't dead yet.

PHOTO COURTESY PETE GERIG

FROM LEFT: Guy Moss, Frank Gerig, Pete Gerig (top hat and debonair), and Charley Gerig. OPPOSITE: Pete's still writing, and composed the poem above to celebrate his one-hundredth birthday. Pete was born in 1893. The Underwood typewriter he uses was manufactured in 1923.

OREGON . SPRING 2005

Ruby Staples, 84

Not a single thing not broken or bent.

Ruby Staples has ridden, "since she could straddle the saddle." At 84, she's still riding. "I guess I was born tough," she says with a smile. In her late seventies, Ruby had a full-time job checking and moving cattle for her neighbors, Alan and Virginia Baltzor. One day while moving cattle, a horned Hereford gored her horse deep into his chest, almost killing him.

Ruby was born on December 25, 1919. Her parents, Ethel and Ambrose Mahre, were musicians at the program that Christmas Eve. They went home at midnight because Ethel wasn't feeling well. Ambrose sent the hired hand to town to get Doc Jones. He changed horses in town, and rode back with the doctor. Ruby had already been born at 3 a.m.

Eighteen months later, Ethel was pregnant with Agnes and too sick to take care of Ruby. Ruby was her daddy's little girl. She went with him while he worked in the shop. After she fell asleep, Ambrose would pack her to the house where her mom would bathe her and put her to bed. When Ruby woke up, the first thing she wanted was her daddy.

Due to severe winters, the Mahre kids started grade school in April and were out before Christmas. During the school year, they got out to help gather cattle, brand, move them to the mountain for the summer, and to help hay. Ruby ran the buckrake. "When we got back to school, we had to work hard to catch up." In those days students recited the Pledge of Allegiance and the Lord's Prayer every morning. They rode their horses to school, each family taking turns bringing soup in a jar.

When Ruby was twelve, she rode a big three-year-old half-thoroughbred buckskin horse in a race. It was hard to see through the dust on the track. Her horse ran into a little gray horse. Ruby won the race but felt like a loser. The men had to take the gray horse off the track and shoot it because it had a broken shoulder. She can't explain how bad she felt that day and she still has nightmares about the race.

Ambrose butchered every week. He would give the neighbors a quarter of beef because there was no way to keep it cold. The beef would be wrapped, put in a shed and covered up with hay during the day. At night, they hung it out. Ruby loved eating steak, biscuits, and gravy for breakfast. "I am still a beef eater," Ruby says, "but now I like a good roast."

After high school Ruby thought about being a nurse, but needed more schooling. Boise, Idaho, was the end of the world as far as Ruby was concerned, so she stayed home. A young man, Jack Staples, lived at the State Line Ranch. He was breaking colts for Ruby's dad. Ruby didn't like Jack. "He never stopped teasing me," Ruby says. They were fifteen and sixteen years old. "We finally grew up, fell in love, and got married a year later," on October 2, 1937. Both mothers were against the marriage, but the fathers said it was okay.

In the summer of 1941, Ruby, Jack and their two kids moved five times between two ranches. They had a team of horses and a freight wagon. "When we moved for the last time, there was not a single thing in the wagon that was not broken or bent." That summer they also bought a Maytag gas-motor washing machine that Ruby "just loved." Before the machine she had used a washboard.

The family was staying at the C Ranch 60 miles from Jordan Valley when the St. Patrick's Day dance rolled around. It was a three-day ride to Jordan Valley. Ruby packed baby Dan on her saddle. Four-year-old Shirley rode her own horse. Jack came later since he had cattle to feed. "It was the highlight of the whole year."

Ruby and her family owned ranches in the Jordan Valley area until her husband died in 1989. "Jack was a good man, a loving husband and father," Ruby says. "He was honest and had no use for dishonesty." They were married for 52 years and had never been apart.

Ruby's life has been incredible, from her surprising Christmas Day birth to moving cattle at age 84 on her little ranch. She has continued ranching on a smaller scale for fifteen years. She goes to church and is a loving person who just happens to have been "born tough."—*Written by cousins Brandan P. Mackenzie and Sonny D. Mackenzie, students in Rena Uhalde's seventh-grade class at Rockville School in Jordan Valley, Oregon.*

PHOTOS COURTESY RUBY STAPLES

CLOCKWISE FROM ABOVE: Ruby astride Buttons on her ranch, with Mac posing in the grass, October 2004. ▪ Ruby and Jack with children Shirley and Dan. ▪ Ruby was "born tough" but with a winsome smile.

NORTH DAKOTA'S ROLLING HILLS AND BADLANDS. PHOTO © LARRY ANGIER

In North Dakota, it was wise to take your cues from the land. That lone treetop in the waves of summer grass was saying something by surviving in a south-facing coulee or a crease. It might be wise to think about it before you chose the spot for your "soddy" and the grass was laid flat by blizzards.

Sid & Doris Connell, 91 & 88

Ranching in the Badlands.

Nestled along the banks of the Little Missouri River in western North Dakota are the Connell Ranch and TIX Ranch. Sid and Doris Connell are the second of five generations who have lived and worked there.

PHOTOS COURTESY CONNELL FAMILY

CLOCKWISE FROM TOP LEFT: Olive and Dan Connell with children: Sid, Lester, Nora and Blanche, ca. 1910. ▪ Sunday afternoon at the TIX Ranch, 1903. Sid's father Dan is at far right. ▪ Dan and Sid's older brother Lester, ca. 1903. ▪ Sid and Doris, 1941. ▪ Doris and Sid in North Dakota today.

Doris was born in Medora in 1912, sixteen miles up the river from the Connell Ranch. Sid was born in 1908 at the TIX Ranch. Both their parents came from Minnesota. Sid's father, Dan, was on his way west to the coast and stopped off in Medora. He never left. In the early years he managed the TIX Ranch, which had been established in the early 1880s during the Texas cattle drives north to the rich short grass of eastern Montana, eastern Wyoming and the western Dakotas. The TIX was named after the famous XIT Ranch in Texas, simply inverting the letters. Doris was teaching school across the river at the Connell Ranch when she and Sid got married in 1941.

Sid and Doris say that the grass in the Badlands is known as some of the best in the world. The nutrients are perfect for making good-looking cows that provide good beefsteaks and hamburgers. They will also tell you that with only around ten inches of annual rainfall, the grasses will still thrive. And when there's drought—like in the 1930s and the 1980s—the grasses will return and the country will look beautiful again.

The pair claim that the love of the land and family have helped keep their healthy outlook on life. A huge garden, which they maintain themselves, their own beef, and keeping active haven't hurt either. "There's the country we care so much for and good neighbors who have helped us through the years, branding, shipping, hauling coal and chopping ice." Reminiscing about the card games and dances at Community Hall brings a sparkle to their eyes.

Sid and Doris' great-grandchildren who are also living on the ranch help their parents with the guest part of the ranch (Dahkotah Lodge). They take visitors on trail rides through the Badlands.

Sid wasn't too excited about seeing his ranch turn into a working dude ranch, but he now says if the ranch is to sustain four generations who live there and future generations they needed to diversify.

When Theodore Roosevelt came to this country to hunt in the late 1800s, he fell in love with the magic of the hills. He called his time ranching in the North Dakota Badlands the romance of his life. The south unit of Theodore Roosevelt National Park is north of Medora where thousands of visitors come each year to enjoy the wildlife and beautiful scenery of the Badlands.

During a recent drive along the river on the ranch, Sid and Doris point out the gap the Medora-Deadwood Stage went through. The headquarters of the TIX was one of the stage stops. The stage ran daily for ten cents a mile and took 36 hours to travel the 215 miles from Medora to Deadwood. There were four stagecoaches: the Kitty, the Dakota, the Deadwood, and the Medora. Now visitors come to Medora to go on stagecoach rides on the river bottoms below the Chateau de Mores. The Marquis de Mores was a wealthy French aristocrat who with his wife Medora, the town's namesake, lived, ranched and hunted in the West at the same time as Roosevelt.

Sid tells of J. W. Follis, who came into the Badlands in the 1880s with a cattle drive and was the foreman of the 777 Ranch from 1888 to 1898, when he became Billings county sheriff. The 777 ran 30,000 head of cattle. Follis was known as a cowboy's cowboy and he was inducted into the National Cowboy Hall of Fame. He died in the 1950s. Sid helped him in 1936 and says, "If I had a tape recorder then, I could've repeated enough stories to write a book."

Follis was a colorful fellow who enjoyed talking about cowboying before fences, when there were long cattle drives to market. "On one such drive from the 777s to Williston, over 100 miles, Follis said they got to the big river [Missouri] crossing and decided they'd just shove the cattle across. Every time the riders would turn back out of the river, the cattle turned back too. The third time, Follis said, 'Come on boys, let's take 'em across.' The horses, by now, were pretty played out. When he got to the middle of the river, his horse quit swimming, just turned over on his side with his nose up out of the water. Follis looked around at those steers and figured he'd have to take one of those critters across. Pretty quick that horse rolled over and went to swimming. His horse was the only one that could get out of the water when they got to the other side. It had been touch and go but they eventually got the cattle to market."—*Kathy "Jess" James*

MONTANA . SUMMER 2008

Mary Jensen, 106

A real marvel.

Mary Jensen is a marvel. On Monday, January 14, the lifelong Hall resident celebrated her 106th birthday, and although she doesn't see as well as she'd like, she has few complaints. She's got a touch of arthritis and needs a bit of aspirin to relieve the pain, but other than that, the cattle rancher takes no medication.

Mary says she gets around pretty good but misses riding horses, which she did all her life until age 101, when her family encouraged her to stop, telling her it probably wasn't a good idea. "She is one of the most amazing people I know," says nineteen-year-old great-grandson Kelly Wilson.

"She was driving her four-wheeler to do ranch chores until she was 103—and at that age she was still driving her pickup and throwing hay out to feed the cows," says another great-grandson, twenty-year-old Blake Hauptman. "Now that is amazing."

Born in 1902, Mary was the sixth child born to Alex and Catherine Wight, who homesteaded in Hall in the late 1800s.

By the time Mary was born, the Wights owned three major ranches in the area, which remain in the family today and are owned and operated by Mary, a grandson, and a great-nephew. One of Mary's great-nieces lives in the original Wight family house.

What Mary loved most growing up in and around Hall was that she could ride her horses everywhere. Of course, she had to—there were no cars in the area for a long while, not until her father came home with Hall's first Model T.

To get to dancing class in Philipsburg, the girls of Hall and Drummond would hop on a little train that serviced the communities.

As Mary grew, so did the valley. She watched workers arrive with draft-horse teams and slowly put in the roadways to accommodate car traffic. And she watched the world change from her ranch in Hall, and from the numerous trips she took overseas.

ABOVE: Mary, left, with sister Ruth and sheepdogs on ranch near Hall, Montana, 1912. RIGHT: Mary and granddaughter Ruth Lindfield on 106th birthday in 2008.

PHOTOS COURTESY JENSEN FAMILY

"She has an amazing attitude—it's one that is always looking forward," says grandson David Hauptman. "She still talks about managing the ranch and the upcoming seasons. And she is always interested in everything going on around her."

These days, Mary's mind is focused on the 2008 presidential race. "There's not a candidate I like," she says. "And I really don't like Hillary. She should stay home and keep to the kitchen."—*Betsy Cohen*

Timber Jack Joe, 89

More than wolf bait.

Last time I saw Timber Jack Joe, he looked to be a hundred years old and was in dubious health—afflicted with lupus, he said. What a pleasant surprise to find out, 25 years later, that the "last mountain man top o' the Rockies" is not only alive but lupus-free. "Turns out what I have is emphysema," he explains. "Yeah, I take oxygen for it, but in liquid form. With my orange juice in the morning." Liquid oxygen? If I were an investigative reporter, I'd demand a clarification.

Timber Jack Joe Lynde was born 89 years ago in a dugout cabin to pioneering parents who rolled into eastern Wyoming in a covered wagon. His father, I.W. Lynde, was a homesteader and a "wolfer" whose method for capturing wolf pups involved tying a rope to little Joe's leg and shoving him headfirst into the den. "I'd get ahold of 'em, and then I'd holler," Joe recalls. "I'd holler anyway, 'cause they was bitin' me, chewin' on me. I'll tell you, I looked like hamburger when I got out of there, but I got every one of 'em."

When he wasn't being served up as wolf bait, little Joe toiled as a shepherd, living in the hills with the flock for ten days at a time. "I got to loving it out-of-doors and I've just always stayed outdoors. I like the wildlife and everything. I like animals. And that's where I really learned to live, when I was herding sheep and being a cowboy."

Following graduation from high school (at the advanced age of 30, he claims), Joe earned his living as a rancher until economic necessity forced him to diversify. He started his own heavy equipment business and went to work blazing trails for exploration companies looking for oil, coal and minerals. He also ran a trapline and contracted with the Forest Service to salvage diseased trees—an occupation from which comes his nickname "Timber Jack."

PHOTOS © RICHARD MENZIES

CLOCKWISE FROM TOP: Timber Jack Joe with a raccoon and a bobcat, at Bearhole 621, a piece of untamed wilderness the full-time mountain man had carved out of downtown Dubois, Wyoming. ▪ At the watering hole with Papoosie in 1974. ▪ Timber Jack Joe in 2000.

At some happy point in time, oil was struck on the Lynde family homestead. What with a steady monthly income from mineral royalties, Joe quickly went from rags to riches—or from rags to buckskins, as it were. Long before it became a popular recreational pursuit, and more than 100 years after it ceased to be a viable career option, Joe Lynde decided to become a mountain man.

He took up residence in Dubois, carving out two acres of untamed wilderness from a previously settled part of town and renaming the place Bearhole 621. There he lived in blissful harmony with his horse, his skunks, his badger, his bobcat, his foxes and owls, and his ever-present canine companion Tuffy. Before long the pair started making public appearances, beginning with the Frontier Days Parade in Cheyenne. With a war whoop and a shot from his Colt .45 pistol, Joe spurred his horse Papoosie and joined in the procession, with Tuffy riding bareback behind him and a skunk named Sweetness cradled in his arms.

Since that day, Timber Jack Joe has been a featured attraction at parades, pageants, festivals, mountain-men rendezvous, historical reenactments, and countless charity benefits. He's acted in Hollywood movies, and rubbed shoulders with Charlton Heston, Robert Redford, Slim Pickens, Willie Nelson, and John Wayne. More than anything else, he cherishes his close association with various Indian tribes and the spiritual kinship he feels with the likes of Kit Carson, Broken Hand Fitzpatrick and John "Liver Eating" Johnson. The fact that his fellow frontiersmen have long since passed into history hasn't diminished Joe's determination to follow in their moccasined tracks.

Sadly, Tuffy has also passed on, although his name still appears in the Gillette phone directory and he remains very much alive in his master's heart. Today Timber Jack Joe has a new canine companion, a collie he calls Lassie Came Home. He's also busy pioneering a new wilderness—an 80-acre hilltop plot nine miles west of Gillette that is rapidly eclipsing Bearhole 621 in terms of quantity of junk and density of wildlife.

"They ran me out of Dubois," the proprietor explains without a trace of bitterness. In Timber Jack Joe's world, there's no room for hard feelings—only positive thoughts and heartfelt gratitude for every golden day that dawns.

"There is just so darn much beauty in everything around me," he laughs. "Everywhere you look, there is God. God is everything. He is not just an image; God is the will to live and do good for others in each of us. All your ways and thoughts—all things are one big circle of wholeness. That is God to me."—*Richard Menzies*

MISSISSIPPI . SUMMER 2006

Tom Wilburn, 87

Exhausting and financially unrewarding.

"Come on up." It's as much a command as an invitation to visitors who stand at the steps of 87-year-old Tom Wilburn's barn-loft apartment. The staircase is steep, the steps are tall, and having to climb them gives visitors an insight into the character and vitality of their host.

Thomas Luther Wilburn, or "Mr. Tom" as he is affectionately known, was born on November 30, 1918, in Columbus, Mississippi, one of four children. He has lived his entire life at Smith Oaks, an 1,800-acre plantation in fertile northeast Mississippi. Tom's parents settled in 1915 on the prosperous farm his mom had inherited.

Tom says, "Dad wasn't really cut out for farming." That fact, along with the onset of the Depression, convinced Tom's father to rent most of the farm and take a job as principal of Prairie Consolidated School. The Wilburn children helped with a garden and the farm animals, and Tom grew to love the horses, cattle, and dogs. His passion was for the work known as "cowboying," which was often exhausting and financially unrewarding.

"One time my friend and I rounded up 25 wild steers that had been roaming on overgrown bottomland. They were so flighty that we could only drive two or three at a time to the railroad pen. The only thing that kept us going was debating how much money we might be paid." The boys got only a disappointing 75 cents each. When asked why they hadn't negotiated the wage in advance, Tom says, "You just didn't do that back then—you were too happy to get the work."

After high school, Tom attended Mississippi State University and studied animal husbandry. He graduated in 1940, completing the final semester by correspondence because he needed to be on the farm for the spring planting. Tom returned the farm to a profitable state. His work ethic and creativity led the sharecroppers and hired hands to respect the young boss who worked beside them and treated them fairly. He learned to appreciate them as well. "The colored men sang as they worked," he says, "accompanied by the soft jangling of the mule chains. I think that's the sweetest music I have ever heard."

In 1942, Tom joined the Air Force and spent three more years in a pilot's pool at Eglin Air Force Base. At the end of the war he found himself back home with enough cash to buy a new tractor and rent the farm from his mother. Much of the land had not been worked in so long that the plow on the brand new tractor could barely skim the top of the earth. "And that was in first gear," says Tom. "Two very wet years followed, and I found myself $5,000 in debt. I tried to negotiate new terms with my sharecroppers and field hands but they all quit."

Tom focused the farm's operation on cattle, hay and corn. As a lark, he purchased a standardbred racehorse and experimented first at local, then at regional races. That purchase started a career of training and driving that lasted 26 years and included 1,800 wins. His success, Tom says, was due in large part to the meticulous records he and his crew kept. "We could look at a horse's card and tell the best way to shoe him, how his bridle should be adjusted, and what sort of a track he preferred."

Tom easily transferred the record concept to his cow-calf operation when he retired from horse training in 1973. He raised cattle successfully for 30 years, receiving the Mississippi Commercial Cattleman of the Year award in 1991. He was one of the first in the area to market his calves through a video auction, and in 1994 he organized some of his neighbors into an alliance, which allowed them to sell their calves by the truckload. Tom currently leases the 500-cow operation to two young men, but he still maintains the cow records and serves as the coordinator for the local alliance.

He's often found on the farm working with his beloved dog, Foxy, by his side. A new hip in 2005 didn't slow him down much, although he says "that physical therapy liked to have killed me." —*Terri Snead*

RIGHT: Tom and Foxy, at the desk where Tom works on records. BELOW: Tom trained champion trotting-horse Midnight Hardy, shown here in the lead and winner of the mile in 1:59.4.

PHOTOS COURTESY WILBURN FAMILY

Roy Junction Road 2 m
John, Sally McBurney 3.6
Barry, Dena Bolton 3m
TIMEC 3m
Brad, Jacque Bolton 3.3
Burt Knapp 5.45
Steve Knapp 6

A CROSSROADS IN RURAL MONTANA. PHOTO © LARRY ANGIER

Some might say they're still shipping cattle to Montana. The Big Sky country wasn't built in an East to West rush. It found its place in a cowboy epic that drove the Texas herds south to north. Even the traditional shape of hats changed as Montana claimed the herds.

MONTANA . FALL 2006

Earl Wolfe, 90

Years of toil have left their mark.

The Wolfe place is just a few miles north of the little town of Corvallis, Montana. It is recognizable by a few head of sheep and some White Park cows grazing in the pastures. From the highway, it looks like any of a dozen or so small farms that still manage to exist up and down the valley floor.

Things on the old place haven't changed much over the years. Ancient tractors and other old farm equipment, treasures not easily abandoned, act as a parts depot to keep the machines that do run working. Rough wooden corrals in need of repair and fencing define the yard. A mound of orange baling twine from the winter's feeding almost buries an old yellow Ford truck behind the tool shed.

PHOTOS COURTESY WOLFE FAMILY

CLOCKWISE FROM TOP: Earl had cattle and sheep, but always preferred the sheep. ▪ Earl and his sheep-herding goose. ▪ Earl, U.S. Army, 1944. ▪ Anna Martin, 1931.

Earl, 90 last May, hospitable and genial, enjoys company and offers a plate of fresh cookies or a pie to visitors that he more than likely baked that morning while watching the early morning farm report. Born and raised on Box Elder Creek near Buffalo, Wyoming, in 1916, Earl moved with his family to St. Ignatius, Montana, when he was nineteen. "We left Wyoming 'cause of the drought," he says. "It just plain dried out. We probably got one crop out of seven years."

Earl enlisted in the Army in 1942 and spent three years in the South Pacific during World War II. Upon his return he signed on as a cook and spent three seasons working for the National Geological Survey, mapping out oil reserves in the northern reaches of Alaska. Out there in the middle of nowhere, he would tell the boys on the crew: "If you don't like my cooking, you can always go across the street."

In 1951, the family moved to the Bitterroot Valley and started running a small cattle operation. In 1954, Earl married Anna Martin, a widow who had a six-year-old son, Walter.

"I always had cattle and sheep but I grew tired of raising cattle. I liked the sheep a little more to work with. If you have your facilities right, why, you can handle quite a few."

Forced to lease pastureland and put up hay on shares, Earl tried different locations before settling in his present place in Victor on the Eastside Highway in 1973. "I was fortunate when I moved here," he says, gesturing to the barn outside. "Why, that was a dairy barn, and they had stalls for their Jersey cows. I converted the stalls into jugs for lambs."

Years of toil have left their mark on farm and farmer alike. With stooped shoulders and gnarled hands, Earl is like a twisted old oak, hardy and amazingly strong. But there is a gleam in his eyes that hints at something youthful deep inside. He only recently agreed to slow down and sell off most of his flock. Anna, his wife and partner of 48 years, passed away in 2002, at the age of 93. Today he works alone, except for occasional help from his sons and a family of close friends who show up for coffee before going out to help with the feeding chores.

"I had to cut down on my work," Earl says. Asked if he was retiring, he hesitates and then says: "Well, probably more lack of help," agreeing that a large flock plus 40 head of cattle was a bit more than he could handle by himself now.

Earl's flock, now down to 70 Romney ewes and two rams, used to number over 300. "The hardest part of being a sheep rancher is probably during the lambing season," he says, "when you're up at night a lot. Lambs don't care about the time of day." Lambing, starting in February, can be the coldest part of the year. "The weather can make it pretty tough on 'em. If it's too cold, the lambs must be kept warm, usually with heat lamps. If the ewe knocks over the lamp, it could burn the barn down."

Earl and men like him are gradually disappearing from our landscape. These men of the greatest generation remain humble, yet they sacrificed so much to keep our country free. With development slowly swallowing up small farms, Earl and old-timers like him are left with a certain sadness that life will probably never be that simple again, and the land, which was once so plentiful and fruitful, becomes something different to those who now live upon it.

Still, Earl's day begins as it always has for the last 90 years or so—with the roosters waking up the sun, and morning chores to be done before the hard work of the day can start...and maybe a short nap after the noon hour when the heat of the day is turned all the way up.

—*Joel Martin-Cox and Walt Martin*

CALIFORNIA . WINTER 2005

D.W. Smith, 82

I liked the suit and white shirt, no dirt.

PHOTOS COURTESY D.W. SMITH

CLOCKWISE FROM TOP: D.W. Smith on McGinny, the beer-drinking mule. He says, "If you wore a big hat in New York City in the 1950s you were a hero. Back then, I could eat three meals in a restaurant and get a hotel room for three bucks."
■ His spoiled dogs never tire of his stories.
■ D.W. with his detailed minisaddles.

He lived every young cowboy-lovin' kid's dream. Born February 6, 1922, in St. Paul, Minnesota, D.W. Smith left home at age sixteen to join a Wild West show. "My brother and I both went into show business but in different directions. He went into ice shows and I went into cowboying. I did everything, tried everything. The contract people in the Wild West shows were performers. They did trick roping, trick riding, bullwhips, knife throwing, fancy shooting, bull riding and clowning. I announced, too. Most of the Wild West shows were back East. "The people in New York City thought we were still fighting Indians here on the West Coast in the 1950s. If you wore a big hat you were a hero while the show was in town. I remember when I was on the road back then I could eat three meals in a restaurant and get a hotel room for three bucks."

When western movies began to lose their popularity and rodeos began to be jackpotted by producers, the Wild West shows ended. "Everyone had to look for greener pastures," he recalls, so he turned to the art of saddle making. "I'm mostly self-taught. A friend of mine was a custom saddle maker and I would stick my nose in anyplace that I could." He also made holsters and bridles. Some of his creations were sold at the old L.A. Horse and Mule Auction in Vernon, California. "We were selling complete fancy bridles for $7.50 and made twenty percent commission… but back then leather wasn't six dollars a square foot either."

D.W. also worked as a ring man taking bids at the auctions. "I think I was the best in the business. I maintained 'make them laugh and they buy,' and I've done some pretty funny things. I could write a book on auctions."

D.W. had a number of saddle shops and did a lot of work out of his garage. For sixteen years he owned and operated D.W. Smith's Saddle and Holster Shop in Mira Loma, California. Besides making saddles, tack and gun holsters, he crafted beautiful exact miniature saddles. His leatherwork and freehand tooling is highly sought after. In 1951 he married Miriam, who passed away in 1997. They raised one daughter, and have one grandson.

D.W. never lost his love of clowning and the energy he received from the audiences. For 30 years he and his miniature mule, McGinny, participated in parades and rodeo events. "When I bought McGinny I could stand and straddle him with my feet flat on the ground and he grew to 46 inches. I thought he was the best mule in the business. McGinny loved to drink beer with me and the guys. The clowns then all had mules. Your rodeo clowns today are not clowns, they're bull fighters. Back then a clown had to do everything or 'goodbye, dear John,' you were down the road. I worked all the parades in California except the Rose Parade. At five miles it was too long for McGinny." The Santa Claus Lane Parade in Hollywood was D.W.'s favorite.

Another lifelong passion is raising racing pigeons. He also raises pygmy pouters. He founded the Western Pouter Club and stays busy raising pigeons.

D.W. lives with three spoiled dogs that never tire of hearing his stories, and one 35-year-old horse. "Last time I got on him, he tossed me in the dirt, but I still miss my Wild West rodeo days. I don't like to stay in one place too long. I'd love to be out on the road right now."

—*Lizett Bond-Jerome*

Herschel 'Hon' Griffin, 90

A man so sweet.

At 90, Herschel "Hon" Griffin still works on his ranch near Riverton, Wyoming. "Not as much as I used to," he says with a toothy grin, "but I try." Hon, still tall and handsome, is for "Honey Bunch," a name that helped toughen him up in school. "My folks called me Honey Bunch because I was just the sweetest thing when I was a baby."

Nicknames were common in the Griffin household. "George was Cot for Cotton Top because he had very black hair. Henry was Pink because of his light skin and reddish-colored hair. My sister Bernice was called Girlie. Gladys was Tom because she was a tomboy. I was the youngest."

In 1906, his father Oliver traveled from Illinois to central Wyoming for the "drawing of lots" in the town of Riverton and the opening of Wind River Indian Reservation land for homesteading. Oliver's draw number was so high he returned home to Viola (with Indian horses to trade), assuming there was no chance for "good" land. In 1914 he read a handbill in the Viola Post Office saying there was room to settle on the reservation. "It said water could be had for 60 cents an acre," Hon says. "You could run cattle on the 'free and open' federal lands nearby."

© C.J. HADLEY

PHOTOS COURTESY HON GRIFFIN

LEFT: Hon in 2002, just a few months before his 91st birthday in July. ABOVE: The family lived in this original sod house that Hon's dad built during the winter of 1915-1916.

Pink, Honey Bunch and Cot in Illinois, ca. 1914. Hon is wearing the dress.

Oliver bought twenty acres of land south of the Big Wind River and built a sod house on the property. It was 1915 when Oliver took his wife Tena and five children, plus farm equipment, chickens, a dog, a mare and a bunch of shorthorn cattle to Riverton in two immigrant train cars. They spent the winter in that sod house and by the following year had added 80 acres and built a new home.

Serious about building a ranch, Oliver filed for a dryland homestead. They received the deed in 1926.

Two years later, Cot moved across to the south side of the Little Wind River onto another farm. "Pink and I joined him to raise livestock and farm on our own." They formed Griffin Bros. Partnership. Later Pink moved on but Hon and Cot's partnership lasted 70 years, until Cot died in 1998.

They built their outfit slowly, using their father's homestead and filing on adjoining land in 1938. "To prove up we each added $800 in improvements, not including a cabin. This was difficult during the Depression but we worked hard, shared everything, and received our deeds for 640 acres each."

Hon married Vesta Lee Boland in 1947 and they moved to a ranch near Arapahoe, Wyoming. They have three children. "The whole family worked together to keep the operation going. With ten kids between us, there were always plenty of cowgirls and cowboys to do the work!"

Hon got his high-school diploma in 1930 while he was working with Cot. He joined FFA when it was just getting started. He received a University of Wyoming football scholarship but chose to stay home and help with the ranch.

What started as two carloads of shorthorn cattle hauled to Wyoming from Illinois in 1915 has become a commercial cattle operation of about 1,000 head of mother cows—now Hereford-Angus cross. They have approximately 12,000 deeded acres and rights to many more acres of BLM land. The ranch supports four families. In 1996, Hon and Cot were named "The 1996 Wyoming Agriculture Citizens of the Year" by the Wyoming Livestock Roundup.

Hon's son Bill runs a ranch close to Pinedale, Wyoming. He says of his dad, "He can still ride a horse or run farm machinery all day long. It's tough to keep up with him."—*Susan Bousman*

Joe & Mary Violini, 94 & 91

Hiding the grappa kegs.

The wind is up at the mouth of the Salinas River where it empties into the Pacific Ocean. Over the sand dunes, California gulls squawk to each other as Joe Violini, 94, and wife Mary, 91, arrive at the family's leased land located near Marina in Monterey County. The home place is the Fatjo Ranch in Salinas, a part of the old Guadalupe Rancho, a Spanish land grant.

PHOTO COURTESY VIOLINI FAMILY

© CAROLYN FOX

ABOVE: Joe and Mary with son Jim, shovel in hand, just like his mom, ca. 1944.
RIGHT: Joe and Mary, age 94 and 91, out for a branding in spring.

Married to Joe for 66 years, Mary takes the ranching life in stride. Today she's driving what the family calls the Lexus "pickup," containing two rolls of barbed wire with the trunk held open by a shovel. Like all ranchers, she does whatever it takes. Joe still considers himself the boss of the operation. He says, "I like to check on the herd."

Son Jim and grandson Scott are doing the roundup work while Mary and Joe watch from the pickup. It's easy to see their wine-glass-shaped brand on the hips of the black bulls. Registered in the 1940s, this replaced the old rib brand in the form of an acorn, which, Joe says, "would stretch out of shape as the cattle grew."

Joe recalls: "My dad was Swiss and bought the big yellow house known as the Cory House. He paid for it with two sacks of gold. That included 1,500 acres of land and a house, which was all redwood, three stories and a basement." That basement, Mary adds, was permeated by "the smell of cooked polenta, and wine fermenting in barrels, and the secret partition in the cellar hiding the grappa kegs."

But Joe insists: "Nothing was secret. It was just a good place to keep the brandy. After all, before they milked the cows morning and evening, they took a little sip to give 'em a little pep."

Joe's dad, also named Joe and very successful, started with milk cows and two dairies down the river road. But when he and his eight siblings were still school-aged, Joe says: "At one point the paid workers left, so we kids had to take over the milking chores." Then, adds Mary, "he'd go to sleep in class." And Joe concludes: "We started to plant lettuce and raise beef cattle. I was the first one out in the morning to help the tractor people. Then in the evening I would go out again. I didn't want the tractor people to work too hard. Farming and cattle—if one is good one year, the other is bad."

Joe was friends with Mary's older brother. "The first time I saw Mary she was carrying a load of schoolbooks."

"We all attended Salinas High School," Mary says. "My family was new in the area, fresh from Roswell, New Mexico."

"First woman I ever slept with," Joe blurts out, getting an elbow in the ribs just as quickly from Mary. To get even, Mary tells on Joe: "Sometimes I'm his wife; sometimes I'm that woman who cooks in the kitchen. I made a quiche for him the other night and he wouldn't touch it—so I gave it to the dog. He wouldn't eat it either."

When asked about the three kids they raised—Jim, Joyce and Annette—Joe and Mary nod in agreement, saying: "The kids just helped whenever we needed help. The kids didn't want to be paid. That was the good old days. Now the grandkids want to be paid. Maybe the four great-grandkids will be different, but if they are like the grandkids, that would be just fine, too."

Before Joe married Mary, they built their own house two miles from the Cory place. "We worked at night by electric light," Mary says. "The neighbors were sure we were up to some hanky-panky.... Oh, don't write that down—some of the neighbors are still alive!"

But that place is gone now, easier to burn it down than move it to make room for the Las Palmas development where they now live. Mary muses: "It would have been perfect for us now." And as for her age, Mary says: "That's nothing—my sister in Idaho is 98!"

—*Carolyn Fox*

CAINEVILLE MESA NEAR HANKSVILLE, UTAH. PHOTO © LARRY ANGIER

Try not to think of history in Utah. Just try to stand in her monumental canyons still strewn with the evidence of others who passed this way long ago before they disappeared, leaving an enigmatic message preserved in caves and soft stone walls that hundreds of dry seasons since have not threatened. You could try not to be humbled by a region so hard to understand. But you had to remember that others had tried before you.

Ray & Herman Vowell, 84, 82

Good times at Steel Swamp.

For Ray and Herman Vowell, life has been a continuum of good cows to rope, enough work to keep them on the run, and a cavvy of horses to ride. The brothers Vowell—Ray is 84, Herman, 82—have made buckarooing a way of life in their years cowboying in southern Oregon and northern California. “I don’t know where we come up with these horses,” says Herman, who’s handier than soft-spoken Ray with words. “I guess we just got it bred in us.”

© LARRY TURNER

The family came to the Klamath Basin in 1910 from Robert Lee, Texas, to a homestead in the Sheepy Ridge area, just south of the Oregon-California state line. They’ve never left, learning the ranching life during summers in and around Poe Valley. “If you went out and worked summers, you got some pay and your board and it helped out Mom,” Herman explains, after noting their father died when he and Ray were only seven and nine years old.

Because Ray was the oldest of six children, he was the first to quit school and work full-time. “Ray saw a bunch of horses go by and he was out of school in the eighth grade.”

The brothers started working for W.C. Dalton at the Pitchfork Ranch in 1937. Since then, they’ve had no other employer. Although both admit that working for a single ranch can be limiting, not allowing cowboys to broaden their knowledge, they believe their years on the rodeo circuit (Herman headed and Ray heeled in team-roping events) and working with neighboring ranches made up the difference. “We were so fortunate,” says Herman. “We worked with good hands. Something less than perfect, they wouldn’t stand for.”

During their years with Dalton, they lived at Steel Swamp, remote far northern California holdings that even today are 28 miles from a paved road. “I’d take a packhorse and come out 28 miles and bring the mail,” remembers Ray.

“I wouldn’t trade those years on that ranch for anything,” says Herman, who lived at Steel Swamp for eighteen years with his first wife, Betty. “Boy, those were golden years, I’ll tell you.”

Herman recalls winters when heavy snows prevented travel in or out for three to five months at a time while he rode horseback on wintering cattle herds.

Along the way the Vowells met up with famed western writer Zane Gray, who lived in the region while gathering information for “Forlorn River” and “Nevada Smith.”

“He was a thorough researcher,” Ray says. “His stories caught the spirit of this sagebrush country.” Herman also remembers seeing California Red, the wild mustang that Gray made famous in “Forlorn River” in 1934, while visiting a ranch near Lower Klamath Lake.

For many years, the brothers ran wild horses on Devil’s Garden in northern California. “Man, there was some tremendous horses,” says Herman, who

PHOTOS COURTESY VOWEL FAMILY

FROM TOP LEFT: Lifelong Oregon cowboys, brothers Ray and Herman Vowell, stand in front of their Malin, Oregon, barn. ▪ Ray with colt he started in 1932. ▪ Herman on Lightfoot, May 1937. The brothers were still riding with the Pitchfork crew in 1998.

can still describe every detail of his favorites. "We knew that country so well we could gather what we wanted to, really good horses." It was a time they miss. "In the early days there was no fences, and in the summer we went from camp to camp with packhorses," he continues. "Gathered fat cows. Branded calves. That Steel Swamp was to me like living in heaven."

"Just being around stock, horses and cattle," says the softly smiling Ray of the lure of life in the saddle, "and breaking horses that turn out good."

For twenty years, Ray and Herman made a name for themselves breaking colts at the Pitchfork and on their own. They're regarded as two extremely savvy horsemen. "It's always a challenge to work a horse and see how much you can get out of him," Herman says. "That was the idea, to make the best horses you could make. That's why you get into it, because there are so many challenges."

Current challenges mainly involve their health. Herman is slowed by hip-replacement operations and laments, "I have to crawl on a fence to get on a horse," but the brothers still have six horses and, without fail, ride with the Pitchfork crew for cattle branding and seasonal cattle drives. Despite physical setbacks they keep busy, offering their ranch corrals for ropings and benefits for handicapped youth. "Our big enjoyment here has been teaching the kids to rope," says Ray, with a broad smile. And Herman brags, "They learn, then later they do really well."

Ray and Herman have worked together since 1937. They've stayed close. Herman's first wife, Betty, who he regards as "really a hand in the roping corral," died in 1966. His second wife, Jean, died in 1995. Since then, the brothers have been living at the Malin, Oregon, ranch they bought in 1963. They take turns feeding the horses and doing chores, but it's usually Ray who cooks the sourdough.

"We feel real fortunate," says Herman, and Ray smiles, nodding his head in agreement.—*Lee Juillerat*

NEVADA . FALL 2002

Leland Arigoni, 91

Abramo Arigoni was a Spanish immigrant who claimed sometimes to be Basque, sometimes Italian. He was jack-of-all-trades: miner, rancher and stonemason, among others. Abramo's wife Angelica was Swiss. They brought three sons with them to the United States, where Leland was born in Globe, Arizona, on November 30, 1911. Two more sons were born in America.

When Leland was eleven, his parents divorced. He never saw his father again. Leland's mother sold the homestead and moved to Cherry Creek and the family was separated. Leland moved in with the Joe May family living on Hot Creek. Joe's wife Fairy was a Shoshone woman who gave Leland a lifelong fondness and respect for Indian culture.

"Mustanging and chasing wild burros was the most exciting thing I ever done. I loved the competition and always went to the biggest and best I could find." Leland's also a great bronc rider. His secret to longevity is that he "never got into smoking or drinking much. Just worked and more or less behaved."—*Nick Tobey*

NEVADA . SPRING 2003

Elaine Smith, 83

Elaine Henderson grew up in California's Mendocino County. There were already four boys in the family when she was born in 1919. Maybe that's why her father insisted that she learn to ride bareback before graduating to a saddle. The family lived by strict rules of behavior which Elaine credits for her strong work ethic and sense of fair play. "If people crossed me, I was ready to fight! Because that's what I did all my life with the boys. They'd blame me for stuff and I'd punch 'em!"—*Clair Hurt*

IDAHO . SUMMER 2003

Archie England, 87

© LEE JUILLERAT

Archie has been around cattle and sheep most of his life. He was only thirteen when he went to work at the Mahaffrey Ranch just south of Salmon, Idaho. "I was quite a bronc rider," he says. "When I was thirteen years old I thought I could ride anything with hair on it, and I pretty much could."

When not working, Archie rodeoed for eight years. "Then I got married, and my wife wouldn't go for it. One day she asked me how I was doing with it, not being able to ride. I told her I'll probably live longer if I give up the bronc riding and stay with you."

Archie remembers his buckaroo years and times in sheep wagons fondly. His rich repertoire of stories includes one about the below-freezing night he found a cow mired in a bog. After yanking the cow free, he spent several frigid hours laying saddle blankets that he'd warmed atop a willow-brush fire on the shivering cow. He says, "I saved that cow."—*Lee Juillerat*

Harris Goldsberry, 89

Bleuchers cost a whole month's wages.

The Badlands of western North Dakota are remote even today. Ninety years ago, when James B. Goldsberry settled some 45 miles north of the cowtown of Medora with his wife Susan and two little children, they were even more remote. Carved out by the Little Missouri River, the canyons, buttes and hardwood draws were a wild place. Neighbors were miles away. But it was ranching country and offered plenty of good range for stock.

PHOTO COURTESY HARRIS GOLDSBERRY

Hunting and trapping coyotes in the Badlands supplemented the ranch income. "Game was not plentiful those years," Harris says. They got to town at least once a year for other supplies.

James had come from Iowa as an orphan boy to North Dakota where he learned to cowboy. One roundup, on the very river bottom that he would later settle, he and some other cowboys were chasing a bunch-quitting steer. They ran him through a small bullberry thicket and flushed out a man clad in furs! He had a little dugout built in the thicket. They never learned much about this old loner—not even his name. From then on he was just known as "Bullberry Charlie."

The family's first home was of logs, built stockade style with a dirt floor. This served until a bigger log cabin was put up where, in March of 1915, Harris was born.

Harris got his schooling in a small log building made by his dad and two neighbors. "We lived off the land, getting to town at least once a year for a few supplies. I worked on my dad's ranch and for other neighboring outfits. I did a lot of hunting and trapping, though game was not plentiful those years."

But Harris' love was horses, and there were plenty of semiwild bunches in the Badlands. He and his brother, Vernon, spent their spare time gathering them.

The unpredictable Little Missouri River can turn unfriendly when swollen in flood. The ice can "go out" unexpectedly, catching the cattle on the far side during calving season. "We could look across the ice-choked stream and see them, but it's 120 miles around to the nearest bridge and back!" Ice jams some years caused flooding over the lower-lying bottoms. After a couple of these episodes, the house and barn were moved back to higher ground.

While the river is a placid trickle most of the time, it can quickly rise from a heavy rain up on its headwaters somewhere in Wyoming. Such was the case on a day that Harry Lowman was working with a team on Goldsberry's side of the river. Harry had driven his team across that morning, but by evening the river had risen.

Harris and Harry had run wild horses together, and Harris watched Harry pull off his new Bleucher boots and stick them upside down on the collar hames to keep them dry while the horses swam the river. After all, a pair of Bleuchers cost a whole month's wages. After a short struggle, Harry persuaded the nervous team to swim. As they jumped in, one boot shook loose and fell in the water near the bank. Harris fished it out with a tree branch before the current swept it away.

When Harry climbed out the far bank he noticed he only had one boot left. What good is one boot? So he threw it into the river—then looked across to where Harris was holding up the missing boot! With a similar gesture, Harris flung it out towards its partner.

When Harris was a young man, cowboys were plentiful, but ladies were scarce until they started coming to teach in the one-room schools. A "school marm" didn't last long before some cowboy "hitched her up." Harris and teacher Margaret Sullivan were married in 1937.

"During the Depression, government land agents came around buying up all the land they could persuade people to sell. It was to be rented back as grazing districts to those ranchers who kept enough of their land to winter their stock on. They said you could rent it cheaper than you could own it. Besides, they promised we could buy it back when times got better. This promise was never kept." Many sold out and left; others sold part of their property and kept just a headquarters.

Harris and Margaret raised three sons: Jerry, Ron and Loren. They added white-faced cattle along with their quarter horses. Electricity came in the '50s and the telephone in 1971. Better roads and four-wheel-drive pickups have shortened trips to town.

When several years of drought forced him to sell down his cowherd, with no hay to put up, Harris and his boys took up team roping. "Back then it was tie hard and fast, throw the steer and tie him down. That was before dally roping came into the country." Harris and Ron won the North Dakota team-roping title in 1961, 1963, and 1967. The name Goldsberry and team roping became synonymous. Never much for show horses, Harris prefers the using kind and his have served him well.

He lost Margaret to illness in 1988. With Ron and Karen and their children—fourth-generation Goldsberrys—on the ranch, Harris helps as he feels like and concentrates on his beloved horses that still follow some of the trails once made by their wild ancestors.

Harris was inducted into the North Dakota Hall of Fame in 2002. He says, "It's nice to be honored for doing something you love to do."—*Jim Lowman*

ARIZONA . WINTER 2008

Mike Landis, 89

Making a washtub out of horse gear.

Mike Landis has done things his way most of his life. For 75 years, this cowboy has stepped into a pair of spur-fitted boots, pulled on his weather-beaten hat, and climbed onto the back of a horse. As Mike sees it, the job of raising cattle has never needed much change.

The son of a Kansas dirt farmer, Mike left home at fourteen to make it on his own. He hitched rides to Texas where he landed a job on a large ranch. From the start, he had a talent for riding horses. And he didn't object to the living conditions the ranch owner offered.

"When I worked on them big outfits in the Texas Panhandle, we didn't get cleaned up from fall 'til Christmas," Mike recalls of those early years. "We didn't consider ourselves filthy. We camped out, ya know? You could make a tub out of a saddle blanket and a horse collar. The saddle blanket would hold water long enough for you to wash up. Now they think they've got to take a shower every week or somethin' ain't right.

"The young fellers of today don't git the opportunity to learn much. Used to be, you would lead a stray cow in. Now they haul 'em in."

Working various jobs at ranches from Nevada to Texas and back, Mike was doing what he loved. He never wanted to be anything other than a cowboy. He says he prefers the company of a horse or cow over that of people.

Mike met his current wife Karen 25 years ago. The couple live on their ranch along historic Route 66 near Peach Springs, Arizona. Karen owned and operated a small convenience store at the site. Mike was a regular customer. "He would come in and buy things," she says. "One day he said, 'Why don't you marry me and come live with me at the Double O? You will have fun every day.'"

Karen did marry Mike, a man nineteen years her senior, and they moved to the Double O Ranch off Interstate 40 where

PHOTOS © JO GRAY

AT TOP: Mike and Karen Landis at their house on the Willows Ranch. Parts of the building date back to the 1880s. ABOVE: Mike rolls a smoke. He says the job of raising cattle has never needed much change.

Mike was employed as ranch foreman. At the time, Mike had no desire to run his own herd. "I prefer to punch cows for somebody else," he says. "It's just easier to let someone else do all the paperwork."

Before long, however, Karen convinced Mike to start his own herd. They leased 110 sections of land in the Black Mountains of Mohave County, Arizona. Known as the Willows Ranch, the site has a spring-fed creek that provides plenty of water for the herd, even during severe drought.

Mike taught Karen about raising cattle. He taught her to ride a horse. He also taught her to rope, brand, and inoculate cattle. Karen taught Mike to share his ranching knowledge with others.

The couple returned to the site where they had met. They turned the building that had served as a store into a cozy home. Then they opened a dude ranch on the property—a different kind of dude ranch—one without frills. Termed a "tent and breakfast," the business provides guests with real day-to-day cowboy work. Guests sleep in tents on the property. They ride horses and work cattle. After a full day's work, they eat at a chuck wagon and tell stories around a campfire.

As word about the no-frills dude ranch spread, Mike and Karen started booking guests a year in advance. It wasn't long before Elderhostel, a not-for-profit travel organization for adults 55 years of age and older, heard of the couple. Mike and Karen signed on as coordinators and the bookings are now done for them.

The guests soon learn a cowboy's life demands physical stamina...something Mike still portrays. Known by many as Arizona's Number One Cowboy, Mike's portrait has been painted by one of the country's leading greeting-card companies. Yet, he remains shy, unassuming and quiet. A smoker since he left home, Mike still rolls his own cigarettes. Buying ready-mades is not an option. Perhaps just another sign of doing things his way.

—*Jo Gray*

SHERMAN COUNTY, OREGON. PHOTO © LARRY ANGIER

The yarns and tales came back from trappers and pathfinders first about Oregon. It was an easy land, but full of contrasts from dark towering forests and rolling plains meeting rivers with the power of the Mississippi. Oregon first, through a low pass into Paradise where the early arrivals were often already waiting as if you were coming home.

SOUTH DAKOTA . SUMMER 2005

Harry Joseph Blue Thunder, 99

Robbing the harvest mouse.

Rancher Harry Joseph Blue Thunder was born May 5, 1906, to John and Annie (White Buffalo Woman) Blue Thunder on the Rosebud Indian Reservation in South Dakota. He grew up in an era of hard times for the Lakota people as they were going through many adjustments from a complete change of lifestyle. The U.S. government enforced the need for Indian children to attend school and would not allow children to attend powwows, presumably to prevent them from learning more about their culture. Harry attended school at St. Francis Mission where children were left throughout the school year.

"There was no TV or movies at that time," Harry says. "Then the flu came. There was no vaccine, no pills, nothing. They just made you stay in bed with no medicine. You just laid there until you were dead. Some of the children died in the dormitory, and the folks would come and take the body home."

Harry was in a coma for four days when his folks came and took him back to camp at Ring Thunder. "The medicine man was there," Harry continues. "He was all the doctor they had then. He saved many lives, including mine."

© PHYLLIS LITTAU

Harry Joseph Blue Thunder was an honored guest at the 2002 Rosebud Sioux Tribal Fair.

"The medicine man was there. He was all the doctor they had then. He saved many lives, including mine."

Harry says they should have closed up the school and allowed the children to get medical help, "but it was much like the Waco, Texas, incident...a good example of policies and procedures that harmed the people they intended to serve."

Two of Harry's sisters died in the flu epidemic at the Bishop Hare School for Girls in Mission. "The police came, then the girls were brought home in a box," he says sadly. "It was rough going at that time."

The family lived in a log house that was heated with a woodstove. They gathered chokecherries, buffalo berries, currants, June berries and raspberries. The berries were ground with a stone grinder, pressed like hamburger patties and laid on a canvas to dry for the winter. They also gathered wild potatoes from the sandbars at the river and would find gallons of wild beans by following a mouse trail to its cache. "We always robbed the harvest mouse," Harry confesses.

The family ate prairie dogs, badgers, coons, squirrels, rabbits, prairie chickens, quail, pheasants, geese and cranes. "We took care of ourselves as best we could," he says. "When a beef was butchered, nothing ever went to waste. It was all dried. The women would take sinew from a place along the backbone and use it for sewing moccasins. I have ate beef all my life and still do."

Harry has always been a man of great faith. In the 1930s, his father gave him two acres of trust land to build a church. Harry held morning services and, during Lent, he rode circuit on horseback spreading the gospel among his people. In 1934, he became a Catholic catechist, teaching people the fundamentals of the Catholic faith.

Perhaps the proudest moment of Harry's life was when he received the Lumen Christi Award from the Catholic Church in 1992. He was flown to Boston to receive it, which was quite an experience for a man who has rarely left the confines of his reservation.—*Yvonne Hollenbeck*

MONTANA . SUMMER 2000

Joe Landa, 90

A Basco in Montana.

On March 15, 1930, twenty-year-old Joseph Landa left his family and Basque homeland in the shadows of the Pyrenees Mountains. He said goodbye to France and St. Jean Pied de Port to board the ship Ile de France at Le Havre. He was heading for the United States of America.

Joe, born February 24, 1910, to Pierre and Jeanne Landa, was the fourth of five children and the first to leave home. He was bound for Buffalo, Wyoming, to herd sheep for his sponsor John Camino, who had paid the $300 to get him there. Like other Basques, Joe would work for free until he had repaid the fare. He spent the next few years tending and lambing sheep on the range and trailing into the Big Horn Mountains to summer them.

In the spring of 1931, Joe's brother Jean Baptiste joined him. Two years later, the pair headed for Bakersfield, California, to work on sheep ranches there. After a short time in the Mojave Desert, they decided to return to the cool Big Horns of Wyoming. They went to Casper and worked on various ranches for about one dollar a day.

"One night the bears stampeded the drop herd and killed most of the lambs," Joe says. "The next afternoon a big brown-colored bear showed up and started chasing a lamb, finally catching him. I went to the sheep wagon and got a .22 high-power rifle the boss had left there. The bear was setting on his hind end with his back to me eating the lamb. He never saw me coming. I aimed between the shoulder blades and pulled the trigger. The bear rolled down the hill like a log."

In the summer of 1934, Joe was in charge of a band of sheep and a cowboy named Charles Burke was in charge of a herd of cattle on the same ranch. The cowboy taught him some English from some catalogs. One was a Hamley and Company saddle catalog. Joe decided to buy a brand new saddle. It cost $94, prepaid.

By the end of 1936, Joe and Jean bought a small band of ewe lambs and made a deal to run them on a sheep ranch where they were working. Two years later, they leased a place on Lower Crazy Woman Creek. Then in February 1941 they leased a place in Powder River County, Montana, from Jim and Kena Catti, who were childless and getting along in age. They wanted to sell the ranch but the brothers couldn't afford it at the time.

The old couple also had matchmaking on their minds. While selling cattle in Belle Fourche, South Dakota, they met some friends from Wyoming. Idolo Giachino and his youngest sister Rosalie were also selling cattle and the Cattis asked Rosalie to come home with them and visit, not mentioning that there were two young sheepherders at the ranch until they were almost home. Well, one thing led to another and on July 6, 1942, Joe and pretty Rosalie were married in Miles City.

In 1943, Joe and Rosalie signed a contract for deed to the Catti ranch. Brother Jean went back to Arvada and bought another ranch. Son Jerry was born in 1944, then Mike in 1948. The sheep were sold in May 1945 at $13 per pair unshorn and Joe switched to cattle because of labor problems and coyotes. Four years later, he added another 2,500 acres to the ranch, bringing its deeded acreage to 11,000. Another 3,600 acres were leased from the state and the Bureau of Land Management.

Joe finally slowed down when he got into his 80s. Even though he has turned the ranch over to his sons, Joe still buys about 80 to 100 yearling steers in the spring. He fattens them on grass through the summer, then sends them to town in October. He still has one permanent head of cattle on the ranch, a longhorn steer that was trailed up from Texas in the drive of '95 from Fort Worth to Miles City.

Joe and Rosalie now live in Broadus and when he gets bored he drives to the ranch and feeds his steer and one ornery yellow cat.—*Jerry Landa*

PHOTOS COURTESY LANDA FAMILY

CLOCKWISE FROM TOP: When Joe gets restless, he goes to the ranch to feed his longhorn steer. ▪ Joe and Rosalie in the early years. ▪ Jean Baptiste and Joe Landa left their Basque homeland in the early '30s. Within a decade, they had purchased land in Montana for raising sheep.

NEW MEXICO . SUMMER 2006

Wayne & Annie Withers, 94 & 89

Maverick steers sold for six cents a pound.

It was 1933 and Wayne Withers had just ridden nine miles from the ranch to get to a country dance in Bingham, New Mexico. It was there he met a pretty redhead, Annie Glover, and on May 19, 1934, she became his bride.

Annie, one of twelve children, came from a farming and dairy family that had moved to New Mexico from West Texas. "They were timid nesters," laughs Wayne.

"My brother and I would get up early and milk twenty cows by hand, clean up the barn and be to school on time," Annie says. "I have milked cows and driven a team since I was nine."

Wayne was raised in what he calls a "sand pile" in southeast New Mexico. "Dad sold that sandy ranch just before they started finding oil and bought a pile of rocks in the Oscuro Mountains in 1923, but the government even took that away."

In that one sentence, Wayne summarizes a lifetime of hard living. He and his two brothers were left to tend the 700 head of cattle while their father looked for better country to buy a ranch. When they moved to the Oscuro Mountains, the Withers' crew built dirt tanks to catch runoff for the cattle to drink. They used fresnos hooked to a team of horses. "It took a lot of time," recalls Wayne. They stocked the ranch with cattle they bought for eight dollars a head and didn't sell any until 1937 because of the Depression. The five- to six-year-old maverick steers weighing 800 to 1,600 pounds sold for six cents a pound.

Wayne and his brother Pat broke and rode horses. They also earned a few extra dollars by rodeoing. "Pat rode bucking horses and I rode bulls so we weren't competing against each other." Annie has her own rodeo memories. Once, dressed in a pair of borrowed boots and bib overalls, she entered the bull riding on a dare and made it to the whistle.

After three years on the Oscuro homestead, Wayne and Annie had a daughter, Dorothy Ann. With Wayne away from home following the cattle, Annie was left with the baby to tend, all the chores and only one horse. Later two more daughters, Margaret and Waynette, were born. "Those girls were the best cowboys in the country," says Wayne proudly. "I rarely had to hire any help as long as those girls were around."

In 1942, the Withers returned from a trip to find the U.S. government had served notice to vacate the ranch. They were given 30 days to move because the area was to be used to test bombs for World War II. "We had a good contract," says Wayne. "They appraised all the improvements and told us we'd get it all back. In 1950 they turned it back to us. We drilled two wells, cleaned the place back up, and then they ran us off again. We were a little more contrary this time. It took them three years to get us off."

The Withers Ranch became part of what is known today as the White Sands Missile Range, home to the testing of the atomic bomb. For twenty years they fought to get their land back, but a federal mandate called the land "condemned to lease." By 1984 the missile range had expanded its boundaries and engulfed a second ranch they had purchased. The Withers had sacrificed two ranches and a lifetime of work to the government. "There wasn't enough left to buy another place, so we just moved to town," Annie says.

This year the Withers will mark their 72nd wedding anniversary. Wayne teases Annie throughout the conversation: "I was only seven when she married me. She took me to raise."

Wayne is a great storyteller. If Annie is nodding, it's a true story. If she shakes her head no, it is not—but her blue eyes, focused on her husband, continue to twinkle. Their love for each other is obviously as solid as the life they have led.

—Julie Carter

CLOCKWISE FROM LEFT: Wayne, Annie and baby Dorothy Ann on the homestead in the Oscuro Mountains. ■ The cowboy crew on the Withers Ranch, left to right: Pat, Wayne, Annie and Jess Withers. ■ Wayne and Annie dancing at their 60th anniversary celebration.

PHOTOS COURTESY WITHERS FAMILY

WYOMING . SPRING 2005

Louise Turk, 83

Dogs wouldn't eat her biscuits.

CLOCKWISE FROM LEFT: Brookie, Louise and daughter Vivian at the mountain sheep camp in 1942. ■ Louise today. She and Brookie began their married lives as sheepherders, living in a twelve-foot-by-six-foot canvas-covered buckboard. During one of the many brutal winters when she would crack the river ice with an ax, she slipped in the water and her pant legs froze hard as stovepipes. "I started to cry," she says. "Lonely times were tough." ■ A Meike sheep wagon, 1941, home to the Turk family.

PHOTOS COURTESY LOUISE TURK

When Helen Louise Hall was a young girl in Kaycee, Wyoming, she dreamed of being out in the hills with a faithful dog and horse, a herd of sheep and a cozy wagon to live in.

At eighteen, she chose sheepherding over housekeeping, and launched her new life with husband Brookie Turk. On that frosty morning in 1941, "I was so excited," says Louise, "I could barely sleep." She clad herself in a plain brown wedding dress and catalog shoes ("too tight to remove"), kissed Brookie, and inked their marriage certificate under the light of a penny match. "My dream was about to come true."

She treasured their late-night dinner in a railroad car converted to a short-order café, paid for "with the last of Brookie's ten dollars," and a honeymoon in bedrolls on the open range. "We were about as broke as two people could be."

Brookie brought 200 Rambouillet sheep up from their Meike Ranch employers that night, and their lives as sheepherders began in a twelve-foot-by-six-foot canvas-covered buckboard. They drove sheep up the Big Horn Mountains to graze in summer. A camp tender hauled the wagons and supplies to the sheepherders in camp, and helped haul everything back down in late fall.

Louise settled into her new home. Under a swinging kerosene lantern were creaking cupboards and sticky drawers, a rickety table (that dumped if you kicked it wrong), a wood-burning stove, and a waist-high straw bed buried in wool and feathers. Saddling horses and hitching wagons two hours before sunrise usually started with a slight nudge from Brookie. "C'mon, kid, three o'clock, up."

"Getting up at the crack of dawn is one thing I never got used to," admits Louise. "But it sure was exciting."

With no land of their own, and wages of $25 a month, the Turks spent two years in the sheep wagon during World War II with a canvas skirt around the wheels to keep out the snow, and a coal stove to keep the fire going all night—on a menu of soup and crackers. "I didn't have the foggiest idea of how to make pie crust, let alone cook," confesses Louise, who says even dogs wouldn't eat her biscuits. "But Brookie never complained one bit."

Working alongside Brookie whenever possible, Louise still chopped wood, filled lanterns, dumped ashes, scrubbed dishes, and lugged pails of water from the river, "with a few places on the trail you could sit and rest."

On cold days, she'd crack the river ice with an ax. Once she slipped twenty feet down the embankment into the water and froze her pant legs hard as stovepipes, yet managed to crawl back to the wagon and collapse next to the hot stove. "Feelings of outrage, indignation, and self-pity swept over me," she says, "and I started to cry. Lonely times were tough."

A rare dance in town or maybe a movie was a four- or five-hour ride to a theater in Midwest (now a ghost town), where they could be "transported into another world," until the curtain dropped and "home" was a wagon, twenty dark miles away over steep trails. "I was just glad I couldn't see," says Louise, who held on long enough to grain the horses, fire breakfast and begin their day without ever going to bed. "I was just glad to be home."

Three winters in the wagon with her newborn baby added to the daily chores, including melting snow to wash and rinse diapers for freeze-drying in the cold wind.

One day baby Pete slipped out of his harness and skidded onto the hot oven, with only minor burns, but moments of sheer terror for parents with "no doctor this side of the mountain."

"The best 41 years of my life were with Brookie," says Louise, who can still gaze across the Powder River at the Big Horn Mountains and remember the wonderful life they shared "under the stars."

After Brookie passed away in 1981, Louise continued to work sheep. In 1998 she retired. Her son, married with three children, lives beside her in Kaycee.

"We began with nothing," says Louise, "too tired to admit the fact we had no money, no job, and no place to live. But we were young, excited about sharing life. Nothing seemed impossible as long as we had each other."—*Gary Watkins*

Long before any mind could remember, vast grasslands of South Dakota rumbled and spoke like a living landscape of buffalo. Too soon, the life-giving spirit of the Sioux, Cheyenne, Kiowa and Crow was piled in huge mounds of pale bones. But now, with greater respect, they have begun to return like such small trees rooted in a forgotten crevice, facing a future of seasons still fierce.

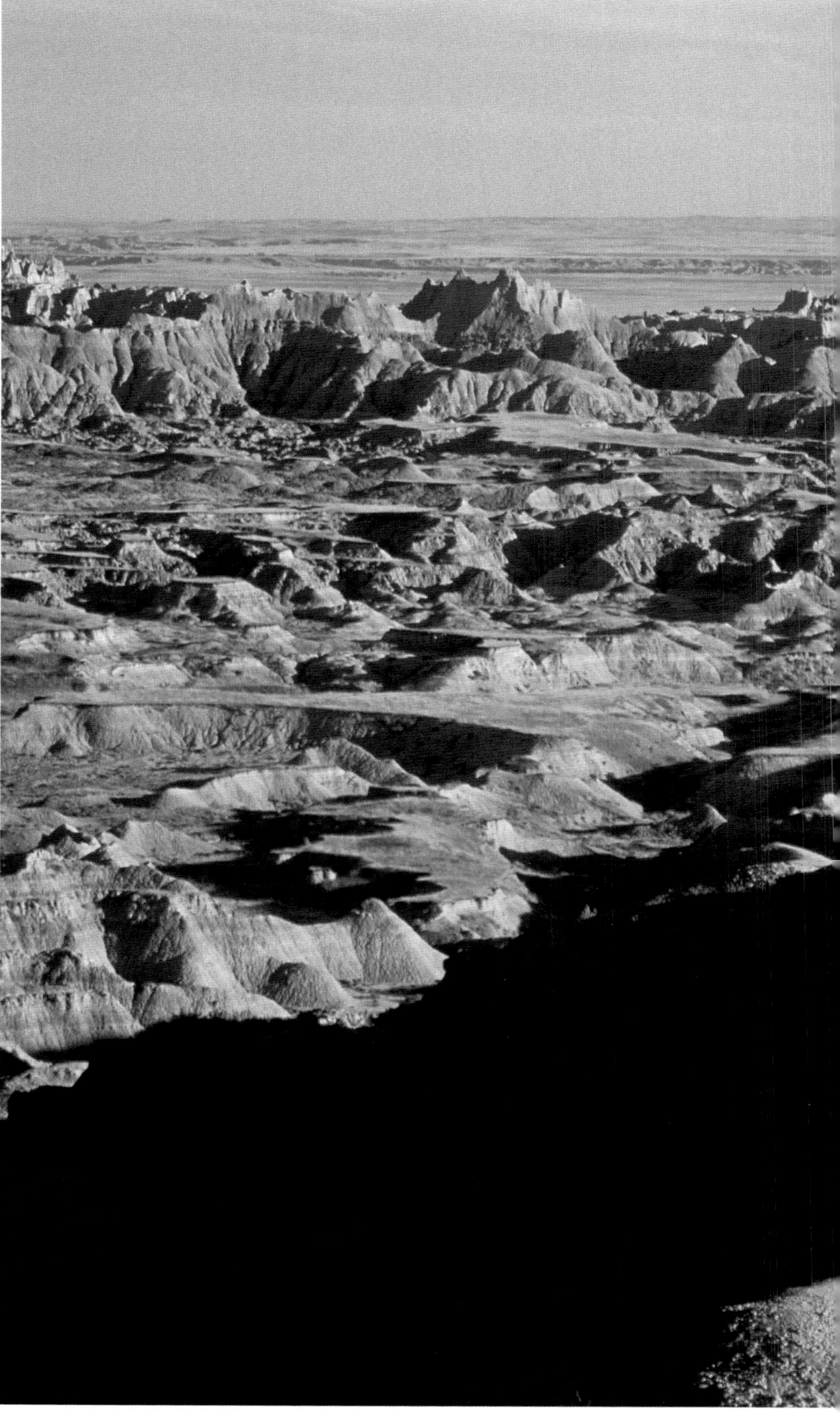

SAGE CREEK AREA OF SOUTH DAKOTA'S BADLANDS. PHOTO © LARRY ANGIER

Lois Roberts, 79

Well fed, watered and content.

Dr. Lois Roberts says that as long as she's "well fed and watered," she'll continue practicing medicine in a remote, rural ranching community in far northeastern California. "I told them that if they did that, I'd be okay," says Lois, who's been a doctor at Surprise Valley Community Hospital and Medical Clinic in Cedarville for fourteen years.

She settled in Cedarville in March 1987 to assist another doctor. Over the years physicians have come and gone, but not Lois. She now shares the load with one doctor and two nurse practitioners and still spends at least one day a week at the clinic. She is on call most nights.

PHOTOS COURTESY LOIS ROBERTS

© LEE JUILLERAT

CLOCKWISE FROM TOP: Lois' graduation photo, 1950, Women's Medical College of Pennsylvania in Philadelphia. ■ Today, with one of the 4,000 newborns she has delivered. ■ Lois mows the grass in Pasadena, California, as a teen.

It was 1950 when she completed school at the Women's Medical College of Pennsylvania in Philadelphia. "Never wanted to do anything else," she says with a smile. "When I was a little girl I wouldn't even play with dolls unless they were sick."

Her half-century in medicine was honored by nearly 300 people during a banquet at the Modoc County Fairgrounds last year. In 1992, she was named Rural Physician of the Year by the California Association of Hospitals and Health Systems. A year later she received the Modoc County Farm Bureau's Distinguished Service Award.

As a rural doctor, Lois says, "You're your own boss. There are no insurance companies looking over your shoulder. No lawyers."

Lois prefers the rural life. Actually, Surprise Valley seems "downtown" after spending 26 years in Africa. "You see just about everything, even some rare things. I don't like the bustle of the city. It is a different life, the rural life...more peaceful. You're your own boss. There are no insurance companies looking over your shoulder. No lawyers."

Actually, the country doctor doesn't like it too quiet. She enjoys the adrenaline rush of emergencies. "I don't sleep through a ringing telephone. It gets interesting when you're on call." Likewise, she brightens at the prospect of challenging cases. "You have to like pathology; you have to like people's medical problems and the fact that you can do something to help them." She has helped with more than 4,000 births. "In obstetrics," she explains, "the interesting thing is you've got two lives in your hand and one of them you've never seen."

Lois speaks Portuguese, which she learned during a year of study in Lisbon. That helps a little with her Mexican patients. "We get along pretty well. They say I speak Spanish like a truck driver," she crows with a rooster-like laugh. "And I probably do."

A world traveler, she's rafted the Amazon and Colorado rivers and gone on archeological digs. Closer to home, for several years she rode horseback while working as a volunteer on trail-maintenance crews and she enjoys fishing and hunting in rural California. Lois has undergone surgery for two knee replacements and an artificial hip. "I never have thought of retiring but I'm breaking apart so much that I might have to."

Medicine is her life, which began August 24, 1922, in Pasadena, California. Most of her childhood was spent in Santa Rosa where her father, John Lewis, was a pharmacist and her mother, Eva Lucinda Lewis, was a nurse.

"I never, ever thought of being a nurse. It was always a doctor. My mother said, 'No, give the orders, kid.' I was encouraged. Throughout my schooling it was never, 'Oh, you're a woman. You can't do that.'"

Lois wanted to see the East Coast, so she went to medical school in Philadelphia. She wanted to live in Africa, so she spent 26 years in the bush in Angola and Ethiopia. She wanted—and still wants—to be relatively free of medical bureaucracy, so she thrives on the remoteness of rural Surprise Valley.

She is well fed, watered and content. "I like the rural practice. More and more I like the people and how they react to their problems. They test you. They finally accepted me," Lois beams. "I still wake up in the morning happy that I'm doing what I'm doing."—*Lee Juillerat*

WASHINGTON . SPRING 1998

Dorothy Simmons, 89

Plenty of hard work to share.

Jim and Dorothy Simmons didn't move very far when they finally sold their ranch home of over 40 years. They reserved quite a few acres to distribute among their children, but also kept a hillside homesite where they built a modern house, complete with a deck overlooking the land. This sustained their growing family for over four decades.

Married for 67 years, Jim and Dorothy met in high school in Wenatchee, Washington. Dorothy was a shy girl of sixteen, and when she was pointed out to the equally bashful farm boy originally from Pueblo, Colorado, he stated firmly, "That's the girl I'm going to marry!"

They tied the knot in 1925 and started out working for area orchardists, Jim pruning and picking and Dorothy sorting and packing, a job she was well prepared to do after being raised on her father's fruit ranch.

Dorothy's hazel eyes sparkle as she remembers how they came to the Methow Valley in 1934. "Apple prices were getting low, so Jim decided to change occupations. We were visiting cousins who were ranching here, and they suggested we rent a 501-acre ranch down the road from their place. They told us, 'You won't get rich, but you won't starve to death, either.'"

At the time they had two children, and after coming to the ranch, another daughter was born. Later, Dorothy's mother and father moved into the turn-of-the-century farmhouse to share the work and the home with the young Simmons family. And there was plenty of hard work to share. The two-story house had no electricity or running water, there were hay fields to flood irrigate and harvest, a large garden to tend, and a burgeoning cowherd. Known as the Dirty Thirties, times were rough all over.

"Most all of the ranchers were charging groceries at the store until fall when they'd sell their cattle and pay their bills," Dorothy remembers. "I raised a big garden, and we had lots of berries. We had twelve milk cows, and I sold the cream to a man in town. We had beef, of course, and I raised chickens for meat and for the eggs."

Jim was responsible for the farming and Dorothy took care of the cattle, with lots of help from her husband when he had time free from his haying chores. "We kept saving the best heifers and would sell the rest of the calf crop, and that would help with the cream check. We had mostly Hereford crosses," she says, "and eventually got some roan Durhams."

After renting for five years, the Simmons bought the scenic benchland which had become their home. They added 1,200 acres of spring range, and purchased a 150-head permit on the Finley Canyon allotment of the Okanogan National Forest.

"We'd drive the cows five miles up to the range. The kids would help, and then I'd go up about once a week to check on them and keep moving them to prevent them from overgrazing."

Was it hard? "Oh, no! It was fun. I always had women who wanted to ride with me, and then my kids and my grandkids would come along. We'd pack blocks of salt up to the Red Shirt Mine. I wish I could be doing it yet."

A horse wreck abruptly ended Dorothy's cowpunching days. She heard that a few of her heifers had gone astray and she saddled her horse to go round them up. As she was chasing them at full speed on the bank of a small lake, her horse slipped on the wet rocks and fell right across her legs. "My arteries and veins were pretty badly mashed, and I was never able to wear my cowboy boots again."

Today, at 89, Dorothy is vibrant and full of good humor. She's lived alone since Jim passed away three years ago. Her mind is crystal clear. "It was a good way to live and raise a family," she says. "We were part of a very close-knit community. During haying, neighbors traded help, and once every two weeks, we'd meet at the old schoolhouse to play cards and visit. It was hard, but we didn't suffer. As I said, I would love to ride yet."—*Virginia Bennett*

© VIRGINIA BENNETT

PHOTOS COURTESY DOT SIMMONS

"Dot," a healthy, active 89-year-old, wearing the same hat she wore to summer range, poses with the 1944 GMC flatbed she used to haul her horses to the Forest Service allotment. LEFT: Dorothy and grandson Steve deliver a salt block to their range cattle in 1965. AT TOP: Dorothy and Jim, married for 67 years, were Grand Marshals at a rodeo in 1985.

Waltzy Elliot, 98

A dollar a day and meat.

There are few who can make the claim of riding for the great Miller & Lux Cattle Company in both Nevada and Oregon. In fact, there is only one—Waltzy Elliott. "I've been a buckaroo my whole life," Waltzy says, a smile on his face and twinkle in his eye. "Of course, in the early years I wasn't paid for it."

Those early years didn't last very long, as Waltzy was drawing a man's wages by the time he was twelve. His exposure to the buckaroo lifestyle began at birth, however, as his parents made a living on a ranch in Harney County, Oregon. His father was a ranch boss and his mother the cook. It wasn't unusual for her to have to cook three meals a day for more than 30 people. Even before he went to work for wages, he had chores to do. "I guess my biggest challenge was milking the cows. You see, they weren't nothing but range cows that looked like they might be milk cows. We had to milk eight or ten a day to get enough milk to take care of the whole ranch."

Waltzy had one brother, Harold, and he was a fair bit older than Waltzy. "I remember this one time, we took the hubs off the wagon wheels so when they tried to drive the wagon away they all fell off. Another time we dumped oil in the pond and began swimming in it. My dad came by and herded us home like we were cattle—and we both were buck naked!"

Before he was a teen, Waltzy was driving wagons with teams and breaking horses for saddle. He was driving horses on a mowing machine when most folks in town didn't know how to put on a bridle. He delayed the eighth grade when he worked for Harry Wilson and Leslie Van Riper, helping them to break colts, riding ten or twelve head every day.

The next year he finished the eighth grade, but opted not to continue school because the cost to his parents was too high. "I decided that was the end of my book learning." But his cowboy learning was about to begin. "Cowboying was a dollar a day," he chuckles. "But you got three good meals along with it."

PHOTO COURTESY WALTZY ELLIOT

A few of the buckaroos of the Miller & Lux outfit. Waltzy is third from right, maybe on Paleface.

As with any cowman, Waltzy owned several really good horses in his lifetime. "There was this one little black horse called Bert that I got from Everett Mickey out of sheep country in eastern Oregon. He handled real nice, and was more than a little bit smart. I sold him to Riley Hough, who was somewhat of an imbiber. Well, he was on the way home one night and was so drunk that he fell off ol' Bert. That horse straddled him and protected him 'til one of the kids came along and got him back in the saddle."

At Silvies Valley Ranch northeast of Burns, Waltzy recalls bringing cattle out of the timber into the flat with a boss named Bill Thompson. Thompson offered the young cowboy a cranky roan horse named Paleface. "I saddled up Paleface and we started goin' down the canyon before we spread out to push the cattle to Harney Valley. All of a sudden Paleface decided he didn't want me there, so he started to buck. He made two jumps, rammed his head into a tree, threw his head up and bucked blind." Waltzy laughs. "Paleface must've thought I did that to him because I rode that horse a lot after that and he never humped again!"

At the end of the year, when the last cattle were driven from the Quinn River Ranch to the stockyards in Winnemucca, the cowboys would get to spend Christmas in town. Waltzy can recall loading cattle all day in freezing weather during the winters of 1924 and 1925. But he also remembers a couple of days of play. Sometimes they would go to a dance, which, in those days, was really something. "Why, you started in the evening and you'd have a midnight supper and dance 'til sunup," Waltzy says. "At Andrews one time, there was a piano player from Burns. His name was Jim Fellows. They had a big dance hall at the back of the hotel and Fellows would set the piano right in the middle of the floor." In every corner of the hall and under the benches were pillows and quilts so the children could sleep while the adults danced. "And they slept," he recalls, with a look of amazement.

If there was no dance, the cowboys would hit all the bars and the red-light district. "Naturally, it didn't take long to spend our money, so a couple of days was plenty."

Waltzy, 98 now, married Gertrude Harnem in 1932, and stayed happily married until she passed away in September of 1972. Today Waltzy lives in Winnemucca, Nevada, where he is enshrined in the Buckaroo Hall of Fame. "I have no idea why I've lived so long," he says with a shake of his head and a grin. "I never did anything special to live longer. In fact, I did everything I wanted to, how I wanted to. I guess I've just been blessed."—*Floyd Allen (2004) and Melanie Supersano and Linda Dufurrena (1992)*

Therlow Leach, 93

Thick with rattlesnakes that killed off colts.

Therlow R. Leach started life 93 years ago in a one-room sod house on a 160-acre North Dakota homestead. The second of six children born into a long line of farmers, he learned at an early age about "the virtues of work, responsibility, dedication and cooperation."

Therlow remembers flat, rocky prairies and severe winters in Minot. His father, Walter Leach, tethered a line between the house and barn on the packed snow to keep the family out of dangerously deep drifts. At age six, there were "long, lonely hours" riding bareback with the task of keeping the cattle out of the unfenced wheat fields. "If I ever fell off," says Therlow, "there was no way to get back on alone."

Despite the harshness of the terrain, the Leach farm prospered and Walter added 200 acres. But Therlow's mother Theodora was unhappy. This was not the life she had expected when Walter wooed her from the college town of Lincoln, Nebraska. To appease his wife, Walter sold the farm in 1910 for a healthy profit and moved the family to a fancy home in Great Falls, Montana. But longing for open spaces, Walter leased and worked the "Junket Place" where he raised alfalfa and potatoes. Theodora and the children stayed in town during the school year. Meanwhile, Walter bought a spread in Sand Coulee. Unfortunately, it was a poor investment. Thick with rattlesnakes that killed off his colts and calves, the Minot profits dwindled and the family moved to the Junket Place.

By 1912, Walter had bought a homesteader's spread in Nashua, Montana. When they got to the front gate, Therlow recalls, "Mother sat down on a suitcase with her head in her hands and was quiet for what seemed like a terrible long time. Then she announced, 'Okay kids, this is it,' got up, went inside, and resolved to make the best of it."

They were there ten years. There was no electricity, no indoor plumbing, no telephone or radio. All travel and farm work was done by horse. The Leaches grew wheat, ran a couple dozen cattle on the range, and raised a few hogs, sheep and chickens. "Life on the farm was always hard, busy, frugal and challenging," says Therlow, "yet filled with the spirit of unity, harmony, love and sacrifice."

The farm was crisscrossed by Porcupine Creek and the Great Northern

PHOTOS COURTESY LEACH FAMILY

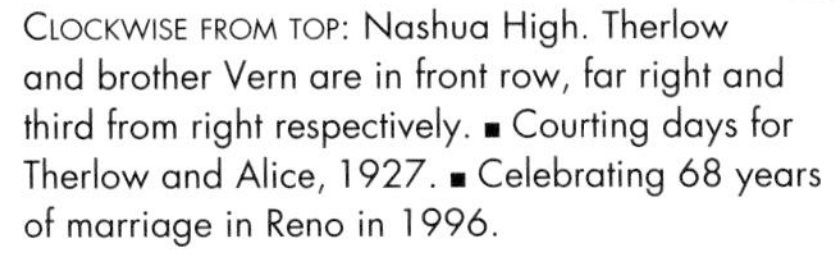

CLOCKWISE FROM TOP: Nashua High. Therlow and brother Vern are in front row, far right and third from right respectively. ▪ Courting days for Therlow and Alice, 1927. ▪ Celebrating 68 years of marriage in Reno in 1996.

Railroad. One horrifying day Therlow's younger brother Richard lost his leg after slipping under the wheels of the train as he tried hopping a ride home from school.

When Walter died suddenly in 1925, Vern, the eldest, finished out his father's term as grain-elevator manager and Therlow ran the farm and single-handedly brought in the wheat crop with a failing horse-drawn harvester. Theodora sold out later that year and moved the family to Bozeman to fulfill her lifelong dream of seeing all of her children finish college. The siblings took turns, except Therlow, who gave up his place in the college rotation to allow Richard to go straight through.

Therlow married Alice Reed in 1928 and became a Star Route mail carrier, earning $125 per month. By 1930 the couple had moved to Thermopolis, Wyoming, where they raised and sold vegetables from a small truck garden. Meanwhile, Therlow entered into an early market corn venture with an uncle on a twenty-acre leased test plot outside of town. The reward was a crop that commanded prices as high as a-dollar-a-dozen ears for two weeks. By the end of the season, however, they were lucky to get a dollar per sack.

With the onset of the Depression, Therlow and his wife couldn't afford their rented home in town and lost the garden that went with it. The young family moved out to the test plot where Therlow had built a twelve-foot-by-sixteen-foot tent house, reinforced with a wooden frame, insulated with cardboard, and heated by slag coal. They resumed truck gardening but economic conditions worsened. What Therlow couldn't sell, he gave away to homeless families or bartered for the things his family needed. Meat came mostly from hunting cottontail rabbits.

By 1937, Therlow resumed his college education in Bozeman. He graduated in 1940 and for the next nineteen years taught vocational agriculture and served as a Future Farmers of America advisor. In 1960, he began working for the Farmer's Home Administration and served for more than twelve years in nine offices and 21 counties in California and Nevada.

Therlow and Alice spent nearly 69 years together and raised four daughters and two sons (one of whom drowned at age two in an irrigation ditch). Alice died in March 1997. "Our lives," Therlow says, "were punctuated with hardship, determination, faith in God, and love for each other."—*Eileen DiCicco*

SAGUARO CACTUS, ARIZONA. PHOTO © LARRY ANGIER

Follow those hard brush trails along border canyons and you might meet remains of Spanish missions or Mexican travelers. The Yaqui and Geromino's own Apache claimed it too. Holding on to what you had or found in Arizona might depend upon making as many friends as possible. Trust was taken seriously in a region that seldom forgave mistakes.

Wayne Wright, 92

A true cowboy never complains.

Wayne Wright enjoys sitting in the sunshine on the front porch of his small frame house nestled in a grove of cottonwoods and located on a back street in Sonoita, Arizona. Gone are the pointy-toed boots, spurs, chaps and wide hats. He is usually dressed in a clean white cowboy shirt, jeans and soft shoes. Across the highway, local calf-roping competitors use the fairgrounds for their practice. Aromas drifting from the stock make him feel right at home.

Wayne comes from hardy pioneer stock. His family homesteaded the rolling prairie sagebrush country of Powell Flats in northern Wyoming, near Cody. He was thirteen years old when he took his first cowboy job, moving a small herd of cattle from Powell Flats up to the open grazing land and the lush grass of Polecat Bench.

Teenaged Wayne was working in Wyoming on a neighbor's place when a stranger rode in driving a two-wheel cart and leading a fancy Morgan horse. The Richardson family took in boarders and the gentleman stayed the night. The next day he put together a race from Powell Flats, Wyoming, to Billings, Montana—exactly 100 miles. Wayne's boss, H.A. Richardson, agreed to the $15 bet and sent Wayne as his rider. Wayne's horse was Old Scarface—twelve years old, not halter-broken, and with an unpredictable wild streak. "You can't ride that old horse for 100 miles. He isn't even wearing any shoes," the stranger said. Wayne explained, "This horse has never worn shoes and his feet are hard as steel."

Several local men joined the race. The next morning at 6 a.m. the race began, with the horses bucking and running. The horsemen headed north, traveling through Warren, Montana, into the Crow Indian Reservation beside the Pryor Mountains and finally crossing the Yellowstone River into Billings. Wayne averaged ten miles per hour and finished the race in exactly ten hours—an hour ahead of his nearest competition. "Old Scarface wasn't even tired." But Wayne was. "That ride is why I walk bowlegged even today."

Riding the horse back was even harder. "Old Scarface was bought by Leo Cramer, who supplied stock to the rodeos. That ornery horse finished his career doing what he liked best, throwing cowboys off his back."

PHOTOS COURTESY WRIGHT FAMILY

CLOCKWISE FROM LEFT: Wayne and Clem, 2003. Wayne was thirteen when he took his first cowboy job. Later, he supplied sheep and horses for a Frank Sinatra movie called "Dirty Dingus McGee." Wayne describes Sinatra simply: "He was a hard man to work with." ▪ Wayne on Little Tommy, Arizona, 1950. ▪ Wayne and Clem are shown here having fun in the late 1970s as Wild West figures.

Wayne's slender wife and partner since 1935, Clementine "Clem" Rassier Wright, has enjoyed all of the good years—and even the rough years of cowboying, rodeos, and farming. They have two sons, John and Kenneth.

In 1948, they received an offer to move to Tucson and manage the horse program for the Arizona School for Boys. Clem says that the harsh Wyoming winters helped to make their decision quickly. Wayne's job was teaching the boys how to ride, rope and play polo. Several times he led the polo team to national victories. His team played in the national competition at Madison Square Garden in New York City. After the school year in Tucson he took his horses to Steamboat Springs, Colorado, for a summer camp. He enjoyed both jobs until he was injured in a bad horse wreck.

After leaving the school, he became foreman of the Apache Springs Ranch in the Santa Rita Mountains north of Sonoita. It was rugged country, with mountain lions, and Wayne spent most of his time in the saddle pasturing brand-new calves and maintaining catch pens scattered around the ranch for the wild cattle.

Wayne never made a lot of money as a cowboy, but his memory of the easiest money he ever made was in supplying the sheep and horses for a Frank Sinatra movie called "Dirty Dingus McGee." Wayne was paid two dollars a head per day, plus a salary for being a wrangler on the movie set. Cowboys are always polite and say a lot with just a few words. Wayne's comment about Frank Sinatra is, "He was a hard man to work with."

Swollen, arthritic hands and aching joints bother Wayne from time to time. All of the hard work of mending fences, roping, and busting wild broncos have come home to roost and now he pays the price. Aches and pains have done nothing to dampen his good humor, though, because a true cowboy never complains.

Wayne is filled with stories of his cowboy days. "By the way, did I ever tell you the story about the time I went hunting with the Lee brothers and roped a mountain lion?"—*Gary Warlick*

NEVADA . SPRING 2002

Lina Sharp, 83

Blue Eagle, Duckwater and Currant.

Although born in Los Angeles in 1919 of Yugoslavian immigrants, most of Lina Sharp's life has been spent in and around Railroad Valley in eastern Nevada. When Lina was about ten, the family moved to Las Vegas. She graduated from the University of Nevada, Reno, in 1940 with a teaching credential, and was given a list of rural schools that needed teachers.

At Blue Eagle Ranch, Lina had to learn how to build a fire in her old miner's cabin. In 1941, after a year of teaching, Lina fell in love and married Jim Sharp. She homeschooled their five daughters. In the 1950s there were enough children to reopen the Blue Eagle School. "Last year we celebrated moving the 100-year-old one-room schoolhouse back to the ranch where I first taught. It's right next to the house here," Lina says. "A friend came up from Las Vegas bringing me a flag with only 48 stars—just like I had in the schoolhouse."

During the years she taught in the remote communities of Blue Eagle, Duckwater and Currant, Lina drove the old school bus-yellow station wagon, picking up nine or ten kids every day. "I went into town each summer to purchase a new set of tires for the school wagon. We had a new school superintendent. 'What do you mean, you bought a new set of tires and gave the old ones away?' he said. 'You must put in a requisition and then you can get the tires. Take back the new tires and have the old tires remounted.'"

"I used the storm as an opportunity to teach."

She never forgot that he said whenever she needed anything, she had to send in a requisition. "One day a screw fell out of the school wagon's sun visor and was lost. I rang up my supervisor. There were other people within earshot. 'Sir, I need a screw.' Then I heard chuckles and realized what I'd just said. The supervisor said I didn't need a requisition for something that small."

During the 1960s and '70s, Lina taught in Tonopah. She stayed there during the week and went home to the Blue Eagle Ranch on the weekends if there wasn't a blizzard. She had 25 to 30 kids in her class. One day it really hailed up a storm. It made an awful racket on the tin roof.

"So I went outside with the kids and we caught some hailstones. Back indoors we cut the stones in half to see the layering. The other teachers just complained about the noise. I used the storm as an opportunity to teach."

One time a little boy in another classroom brought a snake to school. "Take it to Mrs. Sharp!" was all his teacher said. "They sent everything to me," Lina recalls. "The kids loved it."

When she was teaching second-grade economics in Tonopah, they built a model of the town in the middle of the classroom. "We even had the sand dunes. If your dad worked at the airport, then that was what you did. If your mother worked at the bank, then you were a banker."

The paper play money was cut into fractions: four pieces put back together equaled a dollar. One day there was a problem. A boy wanted to get some of his money out of the bank but it was too early for the bank to be open, so he had to wait.

Lina was strict. There was absolutely no sharpening of pencils during class period. But every Friday was gum day. Another time she bought jump ropes. She had the kids jump between arithmetic and reading, then between reading and geography. This kept the active kids from getting bored.

Lina recently spent a few days in Florida visiting her sister. "I wouldn't like to see so much green, not all year. I was anxious to get home and see a little bit of brown."—*Carolyn Fox*

© LARRY ANGIER

PHOTOS COURTESY LINA SHARP

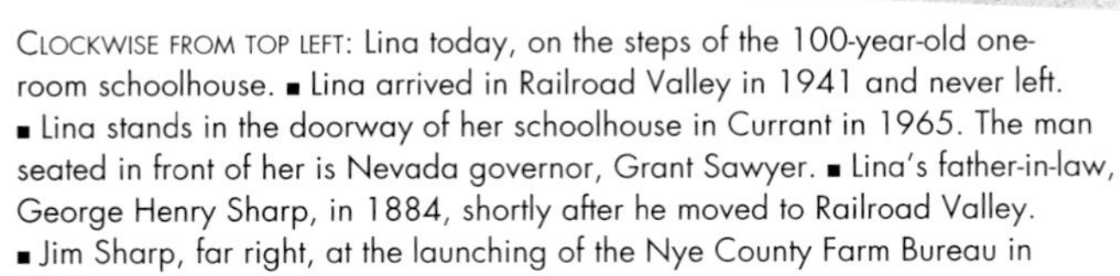

CLOCKWISE FROM TOP LEFT: Lina today, on the steps of the 100-year-old one-room schoolhouse. ▪ Lina arrived in Railroad Valley in 1941 and never left. ▪ Lina stands in the doorway of her schoolhouse in Currant in 1965. The man seated in front of her is Nevada governor, Grant Sawyer. ▪ Lina's father-in-law, George Henry Sharp, in 1884, shortly after he moved to Railroad Valley. ▪ Jim Sharp, far right, at the launching of the Nye County Farm Bureau in 1942.

WYOMING . FALL 2004

Georgie Sicking, 83

A real top hand.

She swings a 40-pound saddle over her quarter-horse mix, hops aboard and pokes towards the center of town to snag the mail. "Ain't nothing," says this Kaycee, Wyoming, horsewoman. At age two, her folks first roped her to a saddle she couldn't slide off. "Broke my first mustang at nine. Heck, I'd still be punching cattle if I could still read the brands."

COURTESY GEORGIE SICKING

Georgie Connell was a five-year-old birthday girl at Trout Creek near Seligman, Arizona, when Dad slapped down $75 for her first horse Buster who loved biscuits. Georgie, in pigtails, wearing Levis held up with a rope, tossed a biscuit on the ground, scooted up Buster's neck and took off. "Just watch out for rattlers," hollered Mom, "and be back before sundown."

Georgie took three-mile shortcuts to school through deep streams and thick cottonwood stands. While the one-room school seemed to teach only "inside work" to girls, her teacher's words, "never say can't," became an inspiration. Whether she was brush-dragged from the saddle, tumbled in a gopher field, or knocked flat in the dirt with a broken arm (after Buster bucked because of a bee sting), the treatment was always, "aw, shucks," and pails of ice water.

"Just wasn't enough cash for docs back then," says Georgie, who talks about having enough horse sense to keep fingers out of a lariat so "you don't lose your thumb like Pa."

Each spring there was a 25-mile backpack into Arizona's Penitentiary Mountains "to visit Dad." There, Georgie, sisters Ida, thirteen, Emma, nine, and brother Clyde, seven, escaped 120-degree heat, broken water coolers, woodstoves and weekly tub baths. Swimming holes abounded, as did sweet pear fruit, cactus candy and squawberries to stuff into saddlebags for lemonade. At night, Georgie sat around the campfires and listened to cowboy stories for hours, "because they were clean and good."

By age seventeen, Dad considered Georgie old enough to run the ranch alone. Her parents had divorced, remarried and moved away. Emma lived with Mom, Ida married, and Clyde got a ranch job, but Georgie couldn't get hired because she was a girl. She shoed, roped, tied cows, packed salt and banged nails until things got lonesome enough to saddle a horse, grab a bedroll and hit the trail to find somebody to talk to. "'Cause now and then," says Georgie, "you need that."

They were cowboys mostly, the kind of people who could be trusted when she had high fever and chest pains, miles from nowhere. Two fellows soaked Georgie's feet in hot water and mustard, wrapped her in warm blankets and stoked coals until her fever broke. "Those cowboys saved my life," she says.

Finally, it was a broncobuster she met at age 23 who she trusted most. Frank Sicking was a real man, according to Georgie, and a real cowboy who wrangled breakfast, scrubbed floors and wrestled the kids when Georgie was out riding herd. He was the kind of guy who doffed his hat, kicked spurs and mud from his boots before stepping inside, and "was always there when the chips were down. Truth is," says Georgie, "Frank and I were partners."

Today Georgie rides her pal Monty along the Powder River into town, where she hitches to the café rail and ropes a few more good clean stories from "the kinda folks who'd never let you down." And for this cowpoke, that's everything.

Georgie was the first Nevada woman inducted into the Cowgirl Hall of Fame for "preserving western heritage through poetry"; honored by Nevada Cattlemen for over 100,000 miles on horseback; and recipient of the Gail Gardner Award for outstanding working-cowboy poet. Author of three books of poetry, Georgie often recites at the National Cowboy Poetry Gathering in Elko, Nevada, an event she shares with one message: "Keep it cowboy and keep it clean."

Today, Georgie lives in Kaycee, Wyoming, with her two horses and claims the secret to a good life is "a good dog, a good horse and a wide open range."—*Gary Watkins*

© CRAIG SAILOR

The "Top Hand" with grandson at her old ranch in Fallon, Nevada. AT TOP: A "Range Rose" at age 19.

ARIZONA . SPRING 2003

Ronald R. Wood Jr., 91

Remembering Pancho Villa.

Like his father, Ronald R. Wood Jr. was born in Chandler, Arizona. It was 1911, a year before statehood. In not the most favorable farming conditions, Ron has spent his life wrestling fruitfulness out of the desert.

Ron's childhood years rushed by as he helped his father run the only dairy farm in Swansea, a mining town (now a ghost town) near Parker. "This was the only time in my rough-handed life I ever got to be a kid."

One overcast afternoon the miners, occupied with pumping water out of a particularly soggy pit, left unguarded a large stack of crates labeled TNT. The boys, a bit restless, thought handling dynamite might be a diverting way to spend an afternoon, so they lifted two cases, dragging them into a nearby gorge. Luckily, after the debris settled and the smoke cleared, no one was hurt. The 800 or so residents were, however, shocked when every window in town spontaneously shattered. But also lucky for the boys. Ron recalls with a wry smile, "The culprits were never apprehended."

As dairy farmers, life was as sweet as the milk they peddled. With a handsome, industrious father playing the part of dashing *lechero* (milkman) to the Mexican immigrant wives, money was flush and they sold the milk faster than they could cool it. In both the morning and evening, the women plodded up the hill with buckets into which "Ronnie" would ladle out his merchandise. There were no government regulations and little overhead. Naturally, it couldn't last. After the mines became too dangerous for the copper they produced, Swansea dried up. Along with all its other inhabitants, Ron father and son blew like tumbleweeds to more profitable parts of the state.

Their new Chandler ranch was demanding, requiring the boy to give up playmates and dynamite for the serious business of becoming an adult. Manly courage would take a few years to develop though, and for a while young Ron preferred a whipping over bringing the cows in when he spied Pancho Villa and his entourage of *dorados* (golden ones) lingering by the headgate.

"Eventually, that compost perfume paid off!"

Legendary outlaws were not the only ones ambling through the streets of Chandler in the 1920s. With less than a mile between the ranch and the San Marcos Hotel, a famous retreat for stars and elected officials, Ron had ample opportunity to get a quick peek at men like President Calvin Coolidge and Jack "The Manassas Mauler" Dempsey. Public figures were less restricted in those days, and he liked to hang about the perimeter of the spread to watch his father offhandedly chat about the farming market with men he was too busy to be impressed by.

But there was more to dairy farming than glamorous meetings with celebrities and flirting with pretty Mexican girls. Being the son of a dairy rancher was less popular in the bustling city of Chandler than in the old mining town. Going straight from milking to school left Ron open to the ridicule of his more urban classmates who ribbed him for smelling like manure. Eventually though, that compost perfume paid off. After moving to the west side to start his family in a shack with no plumbing, he bought his own tiny ranch that ultimately sold for $17 million.

Today, Ronald R. Wood Stadium at Agua Fria High School, twenty years as president of the school board, and the Wood Dairy sign in Swansea are testimonies to the social and historical influence one farmer can have. Who would have guessed that a dusty boy sneaking off to hunt with his friends at Turkey Springs and too shy to accept his future wife's invitation to a weenie roast, would grow to be a successful leader in his community?

Hot and dry as it is, Ron loves life in Arizona. While looking over four generations that have gathered to celebrate his 70th wedding anniversary, he says, "Even an old rancher can make good."—*Megan Basham*

PHOTOS COURTESY RONALD WOOD

CLOCKWISE FROM TOP: Ron's childhood was one of hard work, but "sweet." Hunting was more for food than sport in the lean years. ▪ In November 2001, Ron dances with granddaughter Megan at her wedding. ▪ Ron and his handsome dad.

The Northwest corner, a building block as firm and determined as Washington himself. Yet for all its potential in trade and industry, still a frontier in challenge to the Arctic. Like the other states, and especially those in the West, a place capable with quiet courage of standing on its own. It called for character, and perhaps a bit of wit.

THE PALOUSE GRAIN-GROWING COUNTRY OF EASTERN WASHINGTON FROM STEPTOE BUTTE.
PHOTO © LARRY ANGIER

UTAH . SPRING 2006

Colen H. Sweeten Jr., 86

Perennially short on cash.

Colen H. Sweeten Jr. grew up dirt poor in a place called Holbrook, Idaho, which even in its heyday didn't amount to much. There was a blacksmith shop, general store, grain elevator, flour mill, post office, six-room schoolhouse and a Mormon church. His family, friends and neighbors were strangers to leisure and perennially short on cash. Still, Colen counts himself fortunate.

"As I look back at it," he recalls, "it was a privilege to be raised out there and learn to work. Nobody had any money, but we were all alike."

Today Colen and Ruth, his bride of 61 years, reside in suburban Springville, Utah, but their landscaping includes a couple of Idaho sagebrush plants that Colen claims "followed" him home from his last visit to the Gem State. On the living room wall hang paintings depicting harvest time on the Sweeten homestead, and in the backyard workshop you'll find a scale model of the family barn, corrals and hay derrick. In spirit, the nationally recognized storyteller and cowboy poet hasn't strayed far from his boyhood home.

"Dad, his father, his brothers and some of his sisters homesteaded out there. They bet $16—which was the filing fee—that they could live three years without starving to death on that land. And they were supposed to make use of it, live on it so many months out of the year, and put up their own fences. That's when dry farming was first being experimented with."

With help from his younger brother Warren, Colen's father broke up the first 40 acres with a plow drawn by a team of three mismatched horses and a roan bull. Presently, the romance of dry farming began to wear off, and as one by one his siblings retreated to the city, the elder Colen bought their claims. Eventually the Sweeten spread swelled to 3,000 acres, with 150 head of horses and a 42-foot-tall barn.

> *"When I was a kid,*
> *There was a wolf at the door*
> *Every day of the world, don't you doubt;*
> *Though he was thin,*
> *He didn't try to get in;*
> *He was doin' his best to get out."*
>
> COLEN SWEETEN

In 1932, Colen and his brother George won the contract to bus schoolchildren to Malad, a job that required them to provide their own bus. The nearest thing the two could afford was a secondhand hearse, which they painted Allis Chalmers orange after changing the seating "from horizontal to vertical." Standard equipment included a loaded rifle—in case a coyote or fur-bearing badger should appear in the headlights.

All seven Sweeten brothers served in the military during World War II, and all returned home safely. The Sweetens also fulfilled missions for the Mormon Church, and it was at a religious gathering in San Diego that Colen first spied the girl he would later marry.

Ruth Gerber, an itinerant carpenter's daughter, had grown up in the West and was herself a model of rugged self-reliance. Colen was first impressed by her beauty; second, by her marksmanship. On her first visit to the Sweeten ranch she succeeded in "picking" a flower with a rifle bullet fired from a distance of 50 yards.

PHOTOS COURTESY SWEETEN FAMILY

© RICHARD MENZIES

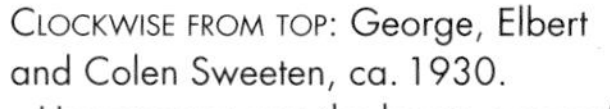

CLOCKWISE FROM TOP: George, Elbert and Colen Sweeten, ca. 1930. ▪ Horsepower was the key to successful homesteading in southern Idaho. Grain was harvested by means of a ten-horsepower threshing machine. ▪ Married 61 years, Ruth and Colen are still in love. He admired her shooting. ▪ Colen is shown here with a scale model of the 42-foot-tall barn, once a landmark in Holbrook.

Colen and Ruth have raised a family of five—"all boys but four." Three years ago their daughter Jan, her husband and daughter were all killed in a collision with a drunk driver. Two grandsons were grievously injured but have since recovered. So have the Sweetens, insofar as they have managed to come to terms with the horrific loss and continue on with their lives.

"I don't give up easy," declares the old cowboy.—*Richard Menzies*

ARIZONA . FALL 2004

Art Dalmolin, 85

Too many flies, an unbearable smell, no screens.

Arthur J. Dalmolin's grandparents came to Globe, Arizona, in the 1880s. Both his grandfather and father were miners and cowpunchers. His father had mining claims in the area and Art worked underground in the mines when he was fourteen years old. Using jackasses and mules, he packed ore from the Round Mountain area to the mining company's chutes about a mile and a half away.

Art and his young friends would hold their own rodeos in the sand washes of Globe. They used jackasses and mules or "any critter that was ornery enough to buck." He broke horses in the Dripping Springs area and did cowboy work on various ranches. He cut wood in the Pinal Mountains and packed it out on jackasses. "This was before they had chainsaws, too."

In the summer of 1934, he and a friend were offered a job herding Angora goats for $10 a month. "We worked only one day. There were too many flies, an unbearable smell, and no screens on the bunkhouse windows."

When the Vanadium Mine closed down in June 1938, Art got a job delivering ice for 40 cents an hour. "Globe was a wide-open town in those days and I delivered ice to four brothels on Broad Street, in the main part of the town. One of the madams was from an old Globe family."

He was working underground at the Christmas Copper Mine when his college coach wrote with an offer of a job for the Forest Service doing "blister rust" control out of Priest River, Idaho, for 50 cents an hour. While doing that, Art also played semipro baseball in Washington, Idaho, and British Columbia, and also played football and boxed for the University of Idaho.

Art worked on the Union Pacific Railroad as a locomotive fireman and engineer during the steam-engine days. He was also a union leader. "As a railroader, my job was considered too important and the military wouldn't take me for World War II," Art says. "But I found a way." He served with the Navy Amphibious Corps in the South Pacific and received a battle star for the Battle of Okinawa.

Art married hometown girl Josephine English. "Everyone called her Jo. She loved to dance and was great at the jitterbug." They have two children, five grandchildren and seven great-grandchildren. He ran a cattle ranch in the Flagstaff area for six years, then the family moved to Oregon in the late 1980s, where he was a commercial fisherman out of Winchester Bay, and gill netted the Umpqua River.

He has been fighting the Bureau of Land Management, the U.S. Forest Service and the environmentalists for twenty years. "I saw how restrictions by government groups and environmentalists were putting people out of work." He wrote letters and attended meetings concerning changes made by these groups which have adversely affected the cattle, mining, logging and fishing industries.

Jo passed away in 1996 after 53 years of marriage, and Art moved to Gold Canyon, Arizona. There he married Emma Reay Rogers, "a cute girl I'd known since 1934. I used to drive from Globe to Winkelman to date her when we were young. Her dad got some wild horses out of Sombrero Butte and some were loose on the San Pedro River. I roped one, tried to ride it bareback and was thrown into some mesquite bushes. I was really scratched up."

He continues to cowboy. In 2002, he was injured while getting ready for roundup on brother Frank's F Bar D Ranch in New Mexico. Doctors put ten screws and three plates in his foot and ankle. "I can't do too much ranch work anymore," he says. "We have the younger ones gather, heel, doctor, brand and cut the livestock now."

Art believes that cattlemen, loggers, miners and fishermen should all stick together. "We should write letters and let our congressmen know what's happening. If they don't agree, we should vote them out."

—*Julian Stone*

Clockwise from top: Art, looking cool and happy in 1919. ▪ Today, on his Arizona spread. ▪ Barefoot in Globe City, Arizona, in 1927. ▪ All dressed up in 1922.

PHOTOS COURTESY ART DALMOLIN

It took time to put up that gate in Idaho, and plenty of hard work too. You had to understand that it wasn't built so much to keep strangers out, but to make it a little easier for them to stop by while keeping the livestock in.

RANCH GATE, SAWTOOTH RANGE, IDAHO. PHOTO © LARRY ANGIER

IDAHO . WINTER 2007

Ben Howard, 84

The old prunes don't want to court.

"The farther up the creek you go, the tougher they get, and I live in the last house!" Ben Howard, 84, is tough! Born July 24, 1922, in Twin Falls, Idaho, Ben's father deserted him, his mother and two sisters when Ben was just eleven. Shortly thereafter, his mother was hit by a drunken driver and killed. The children spent their early years being raised by several different family members.

During his teens, Ben worked for the Utah Construction Company in Nevada, cowboying. "The cowboss offered me $40 a month. I'd been making $50. I said, 'Feller, my arithmetic's better than that.' So I quit."

On June 14, 1944, he married Dorothy Mae Adams of Buhl. They leased a ranch along Three Creeks near the Nevada-Idaho border, then bought a small outfit near Jerome and began building a Black Angus cowherd.

Ben got a letter from Uncle Sam in 1944 that gave him three days to report. "Took my hogs and horses to the Twin Falls sale yard. Got a cent and a half for my horses. I left my one buckskin colt running with my cows. Sold my 60 head of cows to the neighbor on a handshake deal. I got $14 a month in the Navy. Saved just enough out for snoose and sent the rest home to my wife. She was a Rosie Riveter. Got out of the Navy on February 21, 1946. When I got home there wasn't any money left. So I went to check on my cows, since the guy hadn't paid me nothing. He'd put the money in a bank account for me, plus I got interest off it!"

In March 1945, Ben hitchhiked from California to Idaho. He was just in time to see his newborn daughter. Dorothy had moved back to Buhl with her parents.

PHOTOS COURTESY BEN HOWARD

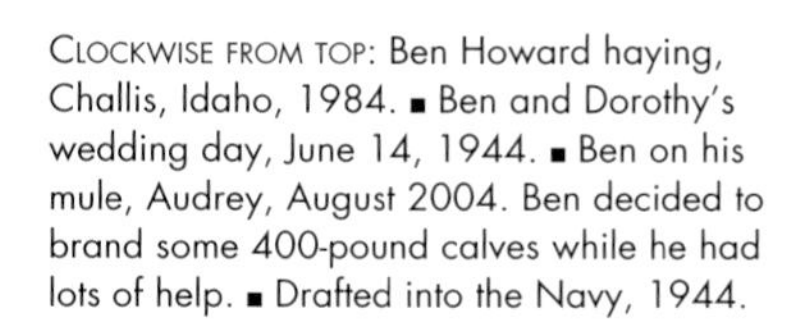

CLOCKWISE FROM TOP: Ben Howard haying, Challis, Idaho, 1984. ▪ Ben and Dorothy's wedding day, June 14, 1944. ▪ Ben on his mule, Audrey, August 2004. Ben decided to brand some 400-pound calves while he had lots of help. ▪ Drafted into the Navy, 1944.

"Come back to Jerome in 1946," says Ben. "Rented 40 acres of farm ground for a thousand dollars. 'Course, my father-in-law's a know-it-all sonovabitch and told me it wasn't worth it. But it had ten acres of popcorn standing on it. So I got a wagon, bought a bronco team of horses, and went to picking it myself. Had to tie ropes to the driving lines to make them longer to keep the damn things from running away. Then I figured out to keep the wagon half full and they wouldn't run off. Made $1,200 off that popcorn."

The Howards moved to Whitebird, Idaho, in 1986. "I bought a band of sheep. Ran right along Seven Devils at the edge of Hell's Canyon. I hired me a herder out of Peru. I herded the sheep right along with him. We hauled the camp on a pack string. We'd go for weeks without seeing people."

Ben enjoyed this life until the Forest Service began giving him trouble about the bighorn sheep. "Those stupid SOBs thought that my sheep made the bighorns sick. But you can't tell the government nothing. They wanted to kick me off my range. I told them to trade me for a cow permit. They gave me one that runs up around Brownlee Reservoir."

Ben couldn't stand the elderly way of life so he and Dorothy went separate ways after more than 40 years of marriage. "If you settle down and don't do nothing, you get old," he says. "I don't want to be old. I want to keep moving. I go to the senior center once in a while. None of those shriveled-up old prunes want to court."

Ben became a gypsy traveling with his cows to different ranges. At age 71, he married Gaylene Hancock. To this union was born a son, Josh. Dorothy treated Josh as one of her grandkids.

Ben still runs cows at his Willow Creek Ranch and lives in the log cabin. He and his dog Smokey make the rounds to see his expanding family throughout the state.

Ben loves to play cards, dance and give helpful advice. He will tell you he only likes two kinds of pie, "hot and cold."

—*Temi Freeman*

TEXAS . FALL 2005

Louis Red 'Bud' Evans, 88

Making doughboys out of mule skinners.

Like the tomb of Tutankhamen, the Texan's home is furnished in a biographical motif. The walls are papered with clippings, letters, citations, magazine pages and photographs, including glossy eight by tens autographed by country singer friends Ernest Tubb and Barbara Mandrell. Horseshoes frame clusters of semiprecious stones. More horseshoes are embedded in handcrafted tabletops.

At the center sits Louis Red "Bud" Evans. Bud's mind is plenty sharp but, after 88 years, the rest of him has begun to show signs of wear and tear. He walks with the aid of a cane and just about every finger points in a different direction. His nose appears to have been realigned as well. For that, Bud has a large quadruped to thank.

"I hit that horse in the belly and I shouldn't never a done it," Bud explains, "'cause he come at me with both feet and knocked me down, broke my nose. So I finished shoein' him—I wanted to finish shoein' him—and went down to the hospital, was gonna go in and have 'em x-ray my nose. But I set there for a little while and I thought, hell, I don't wanna go in there. So I knocked it back over straight—somewhat."

Bud was born in Casper, Wyoming, in 1917, but his father, an oil field worker, soon relocated the family to Willow City, Texas. At sixteen, Bud went to work as a cowboy, buying his first horse for $35 and his first saddle for $10. At the Moss Bar O Ranch near Llano, he learned by trial and error to forge and fit horseshoes, and supplemented his horseshoeing income by entering rodeos. In particular, he remembers a Brahma bull-riding event in Harper, Texas, where nine snorting bulls were on hand but only one rider. Bud took on all nine, one at a time, and limped away nine dollars richer.

"I got paid a dollar apiece for 'em, and in 1935 that was a whole lot of money!"

At the outbreak of World War II, Bud enlisted in the Army. After formal farrier training at Fort Riley, Kansas, he was assigned to the 124th Cavalry Remount Outfit and shipped to Calcutta, India, to break and train horses and mules and teach infantrymen how to manage a pack string. For entertainment, Bud and his fellow livestock wranglers—all former cowboys—organized rodeos that included every event except bull riding, since bulls are considered sacred in Hindu culture.

© RICHARD MENZIES

PHOTOS COURTESY BUD EVANS

CLOCKWISE FROM ABOVE: Bud always got the job done, "no matter what." ■ A cowboy, before he became a war hero. ■ Farrier Bud shows he really does have a way with horses. The horse is even wearing Bud's hat on its hoof.

In 1943, Bud's remount outfit became part of the 5307th Composite Unit, better known as Merrill's Marauders. Commanded by Brig. Gen. Frank Merrill, the Marauders embarked on a 700-mile trek through the mountainous bush of Burma to engage entrenched Japanese forces. Pack mules carried all matériel—including mortars, heavy and light machine guns, ammunition, radio equipment, food and medical supplies. Vastly outnumbered, the Marauders nonetheless managed to disrupt Japanese communication and supply lines and eventually retook Myitkina Airfield, the only all-weather airfield in Burma.

Merrill's Marauders were awarded the Distinguished Unit Citation in July 1944. General Merrill in turn saluted the brave mules and mule skinners. "Next time, give me mule skinners and I'll make doughboys out of them instead of trying to turn doughboys into mule skinners," declared the general.

After the war, Bud settled in Austin, where he worked as a plumber but continued to shoe horses until the early '70s. "I was a horseshoer for 40 years, maybe a little bit more," he recalls. "I had a good reputation of bein' the best horseshoer in the country, and I did a lot of horseshoein', but I got to where I couldn't shoe 'em 'cause I couldn't pick up the shoes or hold a horse up or nothin'. So I took to crawlin'. That's what I did. I crawled."

So next time you gaze upon a statue of a horseback hero, remember Bud Evans, whose gnarled hands and crooked nose bespeak courage, strength, and a steely determination to get the job done no matter what.—*Richard Menzies*

JohnD Winters, 85

Nevada history runs deep.

PHOTOS COURTESY WINTERS FAMILY

CLOCKWISE FROM TOP: Ira Winters, son of John D. Winters. ■ JohnD's parents, Ira and Mary Winters, on their wedding day, January 3, 1904. ■ Lawrence and Bridgett Lynch Kearney, parents of Mary, grandparents of JohnD Winters. ■ Portrait of Theodore, Joseph and John D. Winters, taken in the mid-1800s. BELOW: Kay and JohnD sit on the deck overlooking their Ophir Mill Ranch.

Native Nevadan JohnD Winters is both a gentleman and a rancher. Tall, trim and dapper at 85, he is soft-spoken and gracious—even mellow—when talking about the past and his family. But when the subject shifts to politics, watch out! JohnD turns passionate.

"When I grew up we had respect for our congressmen," JohnD says. "Our politicians felt a responsibility for the people and the country; nowadays very few of them do."

JohnD (not John, or John D., but JohnD) has good reason to be skeptical. When his grandfather, John D. Winters, ran for the office of Nevada's first governor at the height of the Civil War, Winters, a Democrat, garnered the most votes. However, the story goes that because of feared Southern sympathies, President Lincoln didn't want a Democrat elected, so enough votes were tossed out to give his opponent, Henry Blasdel, the nod.

© JACKIE RUFFIN

Even so, JohnD's ancestors achieved prominence in Nevada. Through ventures in mining, politics, ranching, and even racehorses, the family history is liberally dotted with tales of fame and fortune. JohnD's great-grandfather, John Davers Winters, came west via the Oregon Trail in the mid-1800s, ending up ranching in Washoe Valley, a green pocket of land in the shadow of the Sierra Nevada.

Theodore, JohnD's great-uncle, also ranched in the area, but his fame came from his prize-winning racehorses. In 1889, El Rio Rey won the first running of the Eclipse Stakes at Belmont Park, capturing a purse of nearly $24,000. Theodore—once offered a whopping $60,000 for the horse—turned it down.

Mining and politics, rather than ranching, kept JohnD's grandfather busy. In addition to running for governor and serving as territorial representative in Washington, D.C., he made and lost big money mining for gold at the peak of the Comstock mining boom of the 1860s. JohnD's rancher father, Ira, served in the Nevada Legislature for more than twenty years. JohnD, however, was not so inclined. "I didn't care for politics," he says, even though he often worked behind the scenes as a lobbyist on ranch-related issues.

The only son of four children, JohnD was born in 1909 on the home ranch in Carson City to Ira and Mary, a beautiful Irish lass who taught school near Elko, Nevada, before getting married. JohnD spent his boyhood summers at the family's Washoe Valley ranch, where cattle were run from the mountains to the desert, from Marlette to Wabuska.

JohnD recalls how a local ranch hand gave him a Model-T Ford. Hallelujah Bob, after he'd had a few too many, could never understand why his car kept drifting into the ditch on Ash Canyon Road. "One day he came down and said he was stuck again. So I took the horse up and pulled him out. Afterwards, he stopped at the ranch and said, 'JohnD, I'm going to give you this car, but I want you to know there's something wrong with it. Every time I come down that road, it runs into that ditch, so you'll have to be careful.'"

After graduating from the University of Nevada, Reno, in 1932, JohnD worked for the Department of Agriculture and the Highway Department for a few years in Yerington and Eureka. As the Depression deepened, Ira asked his son to come back home to run the 40-cow dairy. JohnD says, "It probably was the only thing that saved us."

The dairy stayed in the family until the 1950s, when JohnD and Kay, his wife of 45 years, built their house overlooking their Ophir Mill Ranch in Dayton, Nevada. The ranch and house are on the site of his grandfather's mill from the mining boom days. From his office, seated at his great-uncle Theodore's desk, JohnD can see alfalfa fields and the cottonwood-lined Carson River. He leases his land for cattle now, and he and Kay see their children at frequent family gatherings. None of their five children, spread across the country, are in ranching. But beef is still important, because he eats it practically every day.

"He's the picture of health for 85, don't you think?" Kay says fondly. "I think he's remarkable." JohnD just smiles and gives credit for his happy life where it's due. "The Lord," he says, "was good to me."—*Jackie Ruffin*

CALIFORNIA . SPRING 2004

Fred & Velma Robison, 81 & 81

Until plumbing was furnished at their homestead in Tulelake Basin in far northeastern California, Fred and Velma (showing chicken to her mother) took summer baths in the irrigation canal. When electricity was finally provided, it went out of service sporadically. So the Robisons traveled down the road and cooked on Jim Stearn's woodstove. "We didn't have roads out here for two years," says Fred. "When we had a dust storm, it just drifted on the linoleum," adds Velma. "It was bad."

—*Lee Juillerat*

CALIFORNIA . WINTER 2005

Andy Giambroni, 81

Fourth of five kids, Andy spent his childhood pretending to be a cowboy. In 1942, at the age of nineteen, he was drafted to serve in World War II. His commanding officer wanted to turn him into a paratrooper, but Andy had other ideas: "I got dizzy standing on two bales of hay." Instead, he became an infantryman.—*Jennifer Giambroni*

OREGON . WINTER 2004

Joel & Marie Peters, 80 & 81

Joel laughs when remembering his chores. "When I was a little guy, I could not wait until I could learn how to milk a cow. It did not take me long to wish I'd never learned."

—*Lee Juillerat*

CALIFORNIA . FALL 2002

Nelle Takacs, 95

Nelle was born January 13, 1907, in Heartland, Washington, where her parents, Robert and Fannie Mae Cheyne, grew wheat. Notes in her dad's diary that day

said, "Baby born. Little Nell. Snowed like hell." Her parents named her Nellie, but as a young woman she chose a new spelling. "I guess I was too lazy to dot the 'I'."—*Lee Juillerat*

Ruth Jeffers, 96

The lessons of Clarks King.

If you thumb through a photo album detailing the 96 years of Ruth Jeffers' life, you'll discover that just about every page is filled with horses. Portraits of horses, photos of horses doing tricks, photos featuring Ruth, her sister Pearl, her daughter or family friends—all on or with horses.

Few photos show people she doesn't remember, and she can name and tell the story of each horse there. Ruth says, "I'm lucky to have a memory as good as I have at my age."

Each horse owns a special place in her memory. They include her first, a former racehorse named Hymn that took her to school and back as a young girl, and on which she raced and beat the older boys. There was Evelyn, that Ruth taught fifteen different tricks; Old Chief, her five-gaited horse that "God had a hand in" by answering her prayer; and the "out of this world" thoroughbred Royal Muse.

PHOTOS COURTESY RUTH JEFFERS

CLOCKWISE FROM TOP: Ruth with Dixie, left, and sister Pearl with Evelyn at 4-H Club Congress in Pullman, Washington, June 13, 1933. ■ Ruth on Old Chief, her six-year-old, five-gaited American Saddlebred, winning his class at Playfair Racetrack in Spokane, October 14, 1945. ■ From left: Ruth's daughter Beth, Ruth, Pearl and Pearl's daughter Donna at the Steptoe Ranch, August 15, 1944.

She had set out at one time to photograph every horse she ever trained. But just as parents take fewer photos with each additional child, it became too much to keep up with, considering she broke and/or trained over 1,000 horses. "I'm not bragging," Ruth says, "but I think I know more about how a horse thinks, and why he does what he does, more than anybody."

Ruth believes horses cannot reason. "If a horse reasoned, you could never handle him, because he's so much bigger and so much stronger than you are. He'd never do anything you wanted him to do if he could reason." She has never found a dyed-in-the-wool cowboy who agrees with her, and she has been known to argue with them until she was "black in the face."

Ruth uses reward and punishment to show the horse what she wants it to do, pausing after the horse submits to give it time to "think" about what it just did.

Her father was Jim Love, and his 620-acre River Ranch along the Palouse River, just south of Colfax, Washington, fashioned Ruth's understanding of horses as a young girl. One horse in particular named Clarks King, was special. "I didn't get anything for training that horse except knowledge, experience and a chance to show him," Ruth says. "But that horse taught me more about horses and animals than anything else ever did."

Clarks King was a brown gelding injured during a race. A local vet rescued him from being put down. Training Clarks King for the vet, Ruth taught him over 30 separate tricks, including firing a gun.

Having owned and operated stables throughout eastern Washington, today Ruth's achievements remain a testament to her training philosophy. These include winning many horse shows, breaking and training horses for others, being one of the first Washington State Horseman judges and five years of teaching riding at Washington State University.

Ruth married horseman William Simpson Jeffers while in her twenties. "I said I will never meet anybody who's as likeable as that," recalls Ruth. "And I never have." They had Elizabeth, their only child, in 1939. But her husband's death from an enlarged heart shortened their marriage to seven and a half years. Ruth never remarried: "Never found anyone else since."

She has lost her balance, no longer rides, and has difficulty getting around. But she continues to remain close to horses. The property that she, her daughter and son-in-law Calvin live on in Newman Lake includes a 50-plus-stall stable where they board, train and lease out stalls to other trainers.

Though she has a cart she can ride out to the stables, she spends most of her time in a motorized chair reading magazines and talking about horses. She remains healthy and strong in mind. A doctor recently informed her that she has the blood pressure of a 25-year-old.

Asked how she has lived this long, Ruth simply states, "I just didn't die."

—*Tim Putnam*

NEBRASKA . FALL 1995

Albert Hebbert, 90

Behind four good horses.

Albert Hebbert remembers when dandelions and nose flies came to the Sandhills of Nebraska. At 90, there's not much Albert doesn't remember about this land he came to when he was four years old. He's watched through floods and drought, wind and snows, and seems to accept whatever happens with interest, not judgment.

"People are always worried about the hills blowing away. I don't know where they think they'll blow to," Albert says, his voice low and slow, emphasizing important syllables. "They used to be nothing but sand, and they stayed right here."

When asked how he came to the Sandhills, and he says, "Behind four good horses." His parents brought up the tail end of the Kincaiders in 1909, settling on a patch of ground south of Gordon. Albert's dad unloaded a wagon full of household goods, staked them down with a tarp, and headed back to Dawes County for lumber to build a shack. Alone on the prairie, he left behind his wife and three little boys, ages three, four and five. "That trip took at least six days," Albert says. That may have been the first time Albert toughed it out in the Sandhills, but it was far from the last.

Albert grew up knowing the hard work of survival. He helped his dad, worked on several ranches around the area, and has seen his share of dangers. When he was eighteen, he single-handedly brought 32 horses through the South Dakota Badlands to the Spade Ranch, a trail he'd never traveled before.

A good chunk of Albert's career was spent well drilling. He drilled over 2,000 water wells in the Sandhills, but he's not interested in talking about business. "It ain't very exciting," he laughs. "The best thing about it was I got to get out and see old friends and make a lot of new ones."

One bright summer morning, Albert meets me at the door with his hat on. "I've got quite a loop planned for us today," he says in his low drawl. We drive north from his home in Ashby, winding through the green hills on our way to the historic Spade Ranch and his early stomping grounds. Along the way, Albert points out wildflowers, native grasses, wildlife and birds. "If you get a chance to look at something, you better look. You may never get another chance."

For every valley, Albert has a story and most carry memory of tragedy or adventure. It was a tough lot that settled the Sandhills. "There's a woman in this valley that was out raking her hay to feed her milk cow. She had a runaway and got drug to death.... Here's a fellow came to homestead—he was trained as a lawyer.... A man over there had a passel of kids and his wife quit him. He went crazy and the kids stayed there." Lone trees on the prairie represent homesteaders he knew who had planted in their optimistic trust.

We turn east and travel through a seemingly endless valley. Grass on either side of the road is taller than my car. Yellow bales sit in the hay fields, ready to be moved for the second cutting. We take a trail road up a hill and stop. Before us lies the valley of the Spade Ranch and trees edge the road and fill the ranch yards. "Close your eyes and imagine it without any trees," he says. "That's how it was."

As much as Albert loves the 'hills and all they hold, the true love of his life was his wife, Ima. She came to the Sandhills to teach in Cherry County in 1925. "It says a lot about her courage," Albert says. "She was eighteen years old and didn't know anyone."

They were married in 1929, and raised five children. "When I met Ima, she didn't weigh 90 pounds. I don't know how long it was before she got to 100. She was a gentle woman." Sadly, Ima passed away last winter. But Albert is far from alone. He's good friends with his nineteen grandchildren, and pictures of his 32 great-grandkids fill his house.

Albert has his own time, a pace a bit slower than most. A friend was power-walking down her country road when Albert happened by in his pickup. He rolled down his window and drawled, "I'll give you a ride, if you're not in a hurry to get there."—*Shannon Dyer*

SHANNON DYER

Albert has a special fondness for birds. "One morning I was with the foreman of a big ranch. I was just a kid. I knew ducks by their silhouette and I knew I saw a spoon-billed duck. That bird was white as snow. I tried to get the foreman to look, but he wouldn't. He had more important things to do. But I watched that old duck and I remember what he looked like. Never seen anything like it again."

TEXAS . FALL 1996

Buck Steiner, 96

Riding bulls backwards.

The Steiner Brangus Ranch sits amongst bright-green grassy slopes spotted with oak and fat, black registered cattle. Thousands of wildflowers, including Texas bluebonnets, show their faces to the sun. Buck Steiner's ranch is beautiful, but it is surrounded by a decadent thicket. "I bought up a lot of broken-down places and it took twenty years to clear it, using bulldozers for all of those years," Buck says. "It seems like I've always been clearing that land!"

Buck likes land. He's bought and sold a lot of it. And he used to lease cattle country as far as Marfa in West Texas. "I finally figured that it would be better to get all my country together in Austin. It was just too much trouble having cattle here, having cattle there."

Buck's son Tommy runs the family's real-estate holdings. Grandson Bobby (who was world champion bull rider in 1973) runs the ranch. "I tell him what to do," Buck brags. "Heck, I rode more bulls backward than my grandson did forwards."

Modesty is not much of an attribute according to Buck. "I have the finest herd of registered Brangus in the United States. They are awful good...." Bermuda grass is native to the area; Buck planted coastal. "Coastal grass is better."

In 1993, he broke his hip and had to move off the ranch. Now he lives close to his saddle shop in Austin. He's in the shop every day, usually with one of his fox terriers on his lap, sometimes answering the phone, bossing around the help when he thinks they need it, telling the craftsmen in the shop upstairs how to make saddles.

Buck's father went broke ranching in Bastrop County. His mother's dad had the first harness and buggy and saddle shop in Austin. Buck's been broke two or three times himself. "But I ain't now," he says with a grin. Even when he was knee-high, he claims to have ridden everything. "I used spools to hitch up eight horny toads to a wagon made out of a matchbox when I was a little bitty kid."

School lost him after the second grade. He left home when he was twelve. "My parents couldn't do nothin' with me. I could pass for sixteen, but I was turned down for active duty in World War I. I'm glad they didn't let me in because just about everybody that tried to join was killed."

Even so, his own life has been kind of a war. He has broken his legs, his shoulders, and his ribs—cowboying. When he was about ten, he started getting on horses and bulls. "I made a lot of money doing it." He earned 50 cents a head riding horses but made real money riding bulls. "At Wild West shows and rodeos they'd always be lookin' for me. I got $25 a head to ride bulls backwards."

He rode bucking horses till he was 59, bulls till he was 52. And he's made money training and selling polo ponies. He says he bought one for $50, trained him, and sold him to a guy in Chicago for $5,000. "Goddamn, he was the most popular horse up there!"

This old cowboy likes women as much as he does horses, mules, land and cattle. "I married the prettiest gal in San Antonio, the only virgin I ever run into, but I just never could settle down. I got a son and a daughter by her and I stayed with her, going back and forth to home for about ten years. Finally I just took off, but I took care of her. I was the best-dressed cowboy on the road and always had a gal traveling with me."

Not known for modesty, Buck Steiner is rightly proud of his ranch near Austin. He raises Angus cattle. "But one-third Brahma in there makes them a lot better." RIGHT: What was decadent thicket, is now pasture. "That took a lot of work."

PHOTOS © C.J. HADLEY

Buck never gives up. He's ridden, performed, stock contracted, supervised saddle makers, cleared scrubland, and been involved in the retail trade and real estate. He has a well-developed appreciation for the good things in life.

"I had some good-lookin' heifers in my life. I did. But now I ain't got a gal but I got my little fox terriers."

He hollers at the help in his Austin saddle shop to answer the phone, then smiles. "I ain't got a gal now, so I sleep with the dogs."—*C.J. Hadley*

MONTANA . FALL 1994

Red Killen, 93

Never give up.

PHOTOS COURTESY RED KILLEN

Moving camp in 1937 at Tongue River. BELOW: Red, ten, his father James, and Old Rover, taken in 1911.

Red Killen talks about Montana when life was hard, the ranches were new, and conditions rough. He emigrated from Ireland in 1923 with five dollars in his pocket and a dream to herd sheep. Today the Killen Ranch outside Miles City, Montana, is a tribute to the tenacity with which Red tackled that dream and built it despite years that tested him with drought, grasshoppers, and volatile prices. He brags a little about how many times he went out of business in those early years. "I didn't fail," he says, "because I didn't give up."

Red is kind of a folk hero in Montana sheep country. He is an old man now at 93, but his yarns told in his native Irish brogue still carry the weight of truth and experience. "I'm the only one left out of the old Irish and Scots that came to this country," he says with a shrug, rolling off names important to Montana's sheep history: Cunningham, Fitzpatrick, Rogers. It was those men who gave Red a chance. "I just wanted to go with the sheep, that's what I told them." Thoughts of that first job still make him chuckle. "They gave me a bedroll, and I was naive. I went looking for the house, but there was no house."

Red left Ireland at 23, to make his fortune in Canada. His family ran about 250 sheep back in Ireland but his father James had been to America some years before, blazing a trail. James returned to Ireland, and his son took up the dream.

"I was heading for Calgary, for I knew there were Irish there, and it's good country too," Red says. But when he took a look at the snowdrifts, he began a trek that took him through many jobs and adventures. He found himself unprepared for temperatures of seventeen degrees below zero. He headed for Miles City with a coat, two loaves of bread and a hunk of cheese, and says he lied to get across the border into the United States.

He walked into a bar on his first day in Montana on May 11, 1923, and he met a man who had worked with his father, and he arranged a herding job for Red with three of the area's sheepmen.

Red tried to leave Miles City once, by buying a suitcase and some clothes and heading for Chicago. He didn't get far, accepting a ride in exchange for work at a ranch, and was quickly convinced by good food and good sheep to stop for a while.

Red tried to convince the rancher to let him run 100 sheep of his own with the larger flock. The rancher refused, Red quit, and he soon partnered up with a pair of Danish sheepmen, buying 600 sheep that later became his. "I ran sheep with some of my neighbors and leased the ranch where we are now."

The country was wide open. It was 1930 when he moved the sheep northeast of Miles City at the start of what was to be a decade-long drought. "It was awful," Red remembers. "We ran out of hay, there was no grass, the sheep had nothing." They sheared and the bank took everything including the sheep wagon. With the banks taking over so many sheep, Red, using money he had saved from the Old Country, took advantage, buying 350 "great ewes" at $3.75 a head. "Sheepmen were going broke in leaps and bounds. Those were days of six-cent wool and four-cent lambs. I stayed in because I couldn't get out."

Red met his wife Stella in 1935. "I told her the truth then, even though maybe I've lied to her a little since," he laughs. "I told her I owed more on those sheep than they were worth. I told her maybe the bank would take it all, and she should maybe change her mind. She said we could start over again if they did."

The couple started married life in a sheep wagon, with Stella tending camp and Red herding the sheep. He credits Stella with starting cattle in the operation, with a cow that had two calves. In 1937, the growing family moved onto the ranch where they now live, buying more cattle and sheep.

For Red, the famed range wars between sheepmen and cattle ranchers didn't apply—but that may have had something to do with his cooking ability at sheep camp, where the cowboys often stopped for chow. An occasional cowboy did fall upon hard times at Red's camp. One cowboy hadn't been too kind to Red but dared to stop for dinner anyway. With a spit into each hand as he kneaded biscuit dough, Red convinced the cowboy to eat elsewhere.

Red eventually built the herd to just under 4,000 ewes. "You can still make money in the sheep business," he says emphatically, and Stella agrees. "It's the sheep that paid off the mortgage for the land," she says. "It was the sheep that brought us out of the hard times."

The wide open ranges Red once knew have been replaced by fenced pastures in many areas, where sheep can graze without a herder. He has watched the large bands of the mid-1900s drop to only a few. Some, he says, were the victims of markets or mistakes, while others simply gave up. "We worked hard and we did good, that's all I can say. We don't owe a dime to anybody."

—*Janice Grauberger*

The sheep will follow the burro and the sound of its bell, always trusting in its instincts to sense danger and see above the sage to another pasture of grass. In their flock, they may seem to ignore the guide, but they will move like a cloud with even playful lambs knowing not to race ahead of the tall-eared creature.

"LET'S GO THIS WAY." BURRO LEADS FLOCK, BILK CREEK MOUNTAINS, NORTHERN NEVADA. PHOTO © LINDA DUFURRENA

COLORADO . SPRING 1998

Norman Ralston, 84

Surrounded at Swede's Gulch.

The sun is sinking over Swede's Gulch. Norman Ralston is relieved to have found his cattle grazing there, under the sheltering limbs of an old weeping willow that anchors the ravine. As he heads back up the steep draw toward home, he stops to rest a moment and laughs quietly to himself. "I just keep going like an old steam engine."

It has been a long day of raking hay, chopping wood and chasing cattle. At 84, most folks would have retired years ago from this kind of physical activity, but Norman enjoys what he does because it keeps him outside and on the land he loves.

PHOTOS COURTESY NORMAN RALSTON

Norman has been living at Swede's Gulch his whole life. Once an empty country, it's now just fifteen minutes from Denver. AT RIGHT: Norman's father Lucian McKeen, center, standing, helped dig this grave near Colorado's Lookout Mountain. It's the grave of Buffalo Bill.

Norman shares his 1,160 acres of rocky, tree-bound ground with 30 head of Hereford and Hereford-Angus cross cattle, an increasing number of elk, a handful of deer and a few coyotes. His ranch has been in the family for nearly a century. Trouble is, the ranch is just a fifteen-minute drive from Denver, which means Norman is under pressure to sell his property for development. The price tag on his land today is estimated at $25,000 to $35,000 an acre, up from the $10 per acre that his ancestors paid for it in the late 1800s.

Many of his original neighbors have already sold out and most of the ranch land that once bordered his property is gone. Recently, a McDonalds and a Wal-Mart were constructed a mile or so from Norman's once remote home. The Colorado Department of Agriculture reports that counties along Colorado's Front Range have lost more than 30 percent of their productive agricultural land to urban development since 1959. In total, the state loses close to 140 square miles of agricultural land to development each year.

Compounding the problem is that many ranchers are senior citizens. "More than half of Colorado's total farmland acreage today is in the hands of farmers and ranchers over the age of 55," says David Carlson, a resource analyst with the Colorado Department of Agriculture, "and 24 percent of the total farms in the state claim a ranch operator over the age of 65."

Norman never married or fathered any children—a disheartening fact, even to him. "I guess the real-estate folks will be happy to have my ranch."

Still, Norman's untouched land remains a port in a storm of change around him.

Norman's grandfather, Lucian Hunter, was a professor at Center College in Kentucky, a government scout and a captain in the Civil War. Lucian's travels brought him to a virtually uninhabited northeast Colorado. "He brought the family to Colorado in 1879," Norman says, "because he liked the country out here."

Still, while many landowning ranchers wage bitter battles and heated debates in defense of open lands, Norman's compassionate, time-tested attitude affords a vastly different approach. In many respects, he seems to embrace the change that is swirling around him.

A hill high above his antler-adorned home—a cabin he calls Summerside—provides a breathtaking view of the surrounding mountains. The recent installation of power and gas lines has left a few thin swaths cleared from the tree-covered hillsides. Asked about these things, Norman replies plainly, "It's for the benefit of many."

But what about the new homes nearby, into which these lines are fed? To Norman, all of this change is a new fact of life. He finds more benefit in acceptance than in argument. New homes mean new friends. New stores bring new conveniences. Power lines signify an end to reading by lamplight. Colorado's Front Range will be a distinctly different place when people like Norman are gone.

As dusk bathes Swede's Gulch in blazing gold and crimson, Norman is well on his way back home. For a moment he pauses to hear the rumble of cars on nearby Interstate 70 and to see the glow from newly built homes. But he understands, and says simply, "Everybody that's born needs a place to live."—*Diane Clow*

IDAHO . SUMMER 1992

Helena Schmidt, 81

The end of the road at Starveout.

She lives at Starveout, 40 miles from the nearest town at the end of a steep, four-mile dirt road complete with switchbacks. The road is challenging when dry, downright hair-raising with a little moisture. But Helena Schmidt, 81 now, remembers when it was just a trail and her family left their touring car at the bottom of the grade and moved everything up to the ranch by a packhorse named Judy. In fact, Helena herself was packed up this trail in the Spring of 1910, shortly after her birth in Weiser, Idaho.

Helena's parents, Friend and Carmeta Moore, homesteaded this isolated piece of Idaho high country and the family lived in a tent until they could get the house built. Logs for the house were cut down from the timber up in the hills and hauled to the building site by horses, guided by her mother. "My parents sacrificed quite a bit for me," Helena says. "It is quite a job to put a kid through school when you live at Starveout!"

When she had to attend high school, the family kept the ranch but moved a few miles out of La Grande, Oregon. Her father worked as a millwright and let Helena use his Model-A Ford to drive back and forth to school. She learned to drive at fourteen, and took passengers so she didn't have to ride alone.

"I remember one day the radiator froze and it started to steam," she recalls. "An older boy who was riding with us got out and put a blanket around it and we were able to get home. My dad fixed cardboard so it wouldn't freeze and after that I always drained the radiator when we got to school and filled it up when it was time to drive home. There was no antifreeze in those days, you know."

Her parents returned to the homestead the year before she finished high school (she boarded out) and when Helena had earned her teaching certificate from Normal College in Bellingham, Washington, she, too, returned to Starveout.

But there was no school near home, so each Monday morning, starting very early, she rode her horse on a four-hour trip from the ranch to teach in a one-room schoolhouse in Heath, Idaho. She stayed with a local family during the week, and returned home each Friday.

© PEGGY HILLMAN

Helena with border collie Ruff. Life has not been easy but Helena admits she got a kick out of the hard work, helping Henry work cattle and taking care of the land. She cooked vegetables from her own garden and used beef whenever they felt they could afford to. "We were often too poor to eat our own meat."

Helena taught for two years, until she married Henry Schmidt in 1927 while he was working at the ranch of Albert Campbell. A year later, they moved back to the homestead to help her parents. Shortly after that, they went into debt to acquire some land at No Business and Wildhorse—two ranches nearby. They lived on all three places, putting up wild hay and alfalfa and moving cattle as the hay gave out. "We always figured to be in the lower place during spring calving," she explains. "It had south-facing slopes and wasn't so wintry."

They never had more than a hundred cows and about four bulls. They moved cows, horseback, with old cows leading the others. "But, of course, when cows get down into draws and under cliffs, we'd have to go in on foot."

Since Henry's death, Helena has lived on the family homestead, now shared with another couple. She heats the house with the woodstove Henry bought for her mother in 1947, cooks and refrigerates with propane. "We bring 55-gallon barrels from town, pump them into a 500-gallon tank. This also runs the generator for the lights and TV."

Life has not been easy, but Helena admits she got a kick out of the hard work, helping Henry work cattle and taking care of the land. She cooked vegetables from her own garden. She used beef whenever they felt they could afford to, but she admits they were often too poor to eat their own meat.

Helena continues to live a long way from nowhere. Occasionally she drives to Council or Boise, Idaho, in her red Subaru to visit friends but mostly she stays at Starveout tending to three cows and a dozen chickens. "We just butchered the bull for meat and a coyote got the rooster." She continues to grow her own vegetables, and her constant companion is a border collie named Ruff. She gets visitors whenever they can stand the journey to the end of her often impassable road.

Even though Helena believes a lot of folks' aim is to move to town, she finds the thought peculiar. She scratches Ruff's neck and looks at the mountains outside her window. "Moving to town," she says quietly. "Now that's not my idea of a good time."—*Peggy Hillman*

OREGON . FALL 2008

Monica Kinnel, 100

Chasing cattle from the crib.

Monica (Ruhl) Kinnel has chased cattle from the crib. This grand gal comes from good stock and June 2, 2008, marked the 100th year of her remarkable journey.

In 1892 Henry and Anna Ruhl purchased 388 acres for $10,000 and assumption of a $2,500 debt. The property sits on the outskirts of Alicel, Oregon, a mountain valley in the northeastern corner of the state. This was to become the seminal grounds for a ranching/farming family that has spanned five generations in the Grande Ronde Valley.

Monica was born June 2, 1908, in the ranch house built by her father-in-law Henry Ruhl. The original home still stands.

"Old Bill, our horse," Monica remembers, "would pasture on Mount Harris for the summer and would come down by himself to take my older brother Charles and me to school in the fall. He just knew it was time to come home."

During her high school years, Monica attended the Girls Polytechnic School in Portland, Oregon, and studied domestic art, domestic science, design, English, history and gym.

"She was a real flapper and I looked up to her," says her cousin Betty. Nevertheless, the saying is true that you can take the girl out of the country but you can't take the country out of the girl. Monica completed her studies, then went fishing. She speaks fondly of her childhood days on the ranch. "We would hunt eggs like a treasure because Mom let the chickens roost wherever they wanted."

Some of her favorite pastimes were playing down by the river. She hunted ducks with her favorite shepherd dog Heinz in tow. Monica says, "animals weren't born grown," so she spent much of her time taking care of them. She had many pets: mice, skunks, bats and flying squirrels.

She remembers anticipating the yearly return of the waterfowl to nest. "I could feel them coming back weeks before they appeared. Mom and I would lay trapline for mink and muskrat down at the river slough. We used some pelts for coat collars and others we sold for fun money to buy frivolous things that a teenage girl needs—like red shoes."

PHOTOS COURTESY KINNEL FAMILY

FROM TOP: Monica, Emerson and Barry on faithful family horse. ▪ Monica holds the workhorses and Heinz the dog. ▪ Monica the flapper wears trapline-caught fur on collar of her coat.

In her early twenties, Monica married Bob Kinnel, who took over the ranch, raising Hereford cattle and farming. They added more farmland adjacent to the Ruhl Ranch and the whole thing became the Kinnel Ranch. They fattened cattle and shipped them to the Portland market by rail, fetching eight cents a pound in 1938. "I rode my horse to take messages to the field," says Monica, "and many times drove the derrick to put up the hay." Together they reared three daughters.

Bob died at the age of 43 in 1955 but their kids rallied around Monica to help run the ranch. Her youngest daughter Sharon married Bob Beck and together they've spent over 50 years adding to the ranch and raising the next generation in its succession.

On turning 100, Monica chuckles, "It was just an accident."—*Toni Burton*

CALIFORNIA . FALL 2008

James E. Wolter, 83

Wisecracker on a starvation outfit.

Born March 10, 1925, in Pacific Grove, California, Jim E. was raised in nearby Carmel Valley. His dad was a dryland hay farmer who raised and sold hay to the Monterey Presidio as feed for the cavalry horses.

Jim joined the hay crew at age thirteen, traveling up and down the Salinas Valley for the six-week season. All the equipment including a water truck for the horses moved together, followed by a cook house. He says, "We had five meals a day cooked on a woodstove."

The hay crew worked dawn to dark six days a week. Handling up to 22 mostly Belgian or Percheron horses, Jim's job required him to change the teams on the "power" of the baler (the derrick that pulled hay up to the baler). "The power horses went on the run," says Jim. "They had to be changed every twenty bales. This was the hardest work I've ever done, but I loved it." Paid by the ton, the salary was about $2.50 a day plus meals. "It was good money at the time."

Jim worked for Berta Brothers in Carmel Valley and also on the Tularcitos Ranch (now called Rana Creek Ranch). The Tularcitos was owned by John Marble of the 71 Ranch in Nevada. "John ran his weaner calves on the Tularcitos and there were a lot of them." The calves would arrive in November-December each year and Jim would watch the convoy of cattle trucks coming over the Laureles Grade from his childhood home in Carmel Village. "Oh, what a sight!" says Jim.

After serving in the Navy, Jim returned to Carmel Valley. The Berta Brothers had "got modern." They bought a pull harvester that they pulled with a wide-gauge D2 Cat. "My boss Leo Berta was a hurry-up guy. When I was working for Berta, working cattle was like being on vacation."

Jim married Janet Larson of Oakland, California, on October 27, 1950, and she has been his best girl for 57 years. "We spent our honeymoon at the Cow Palace."

Purchasing their first cows in 1950, Jim leased the Ford Ranch (now Garland Park) and paid about $50 a month for 900 acres. "It was a starvation place, but you could get by on venison and steelhead." In those early years, Jim and Janet farmed, ran a few cows and even tried raising hogs. Jim claims, "That's when we really tried to go broke."

After being taught to run a Cat dozer by Frank DeAmaral, Jim purchased his first tractor, becoming an owner/operator for about 25 years. Sometimes working his tractor for the California Division of Forestry on big fires that he calls "steak fires" (because they fed you so well), Jim particularly remembers a terrible fire that happened on the Chipinos Ranch belonging to Bob and Betty Wilson. He was working a job in a nearby canyon and saw smoke. So he headed his dozer toward the fire, building a road as he went.

"I met up with Bob on his International but the wind changed, and the fire was really sucking up to us." The men kept going with blades down, but the flames were right on their tails. "I crossed a gully and got into a big field of wild oats. When I looked back, I could hear Bob's tractor, but I couldn't see him in all the smoke and flames. This was the most awful feeling of my life—worse than wartime—knowing that Bob was back there, and I couldn't get to him."

When Bob finally came into sight, Jim flagged down a highway patrol officer who put Bob into the patrol car. "I went back to the dozer and went on cutting a line in the oats," Jim says. Bob Wilson, hospitalized and badly burned, credits Jim E. with saving his life.

These days Jim sits out on his deck in a place that he and Janet call Casa de Adin. If you're driving a cattle truck, headed up Highway 395, look toward Adin Heights as you go through town and give Jim a wave—he'll be watching for you.

—Robin Sachau

CLOCKWISE FROM LEFT: Jim and Janet, March 2005. ▪ Father Joe Wolter on the hay wagon, Carmel, California, 1925. ▪ Brother Dean pushes Jim in the wagon, 1926.

PHOTOS COURTESY WOLTER FAMILY

NEBRASKA . SPRING 1994

Ruby Stedry, 79

Out there, in the wind.

Ruby Charbonneau Christopher Stedry will be 80 this July. She is the youngest and only surviving child of a French father with a famous last name and a Rosebud Sioux mother 22 years his junior. Ruby doesn't quite measure five feet tall, but her throaty chuckle and forthright, determined manner make her seem somehow taller.

She grew up on the edge of some of the wealthiest cattle country in North America, and on the edge of two cultures that had, within her parent's generation, clashed as ferociously over that land as any warring nations. Ruby does not dwell on the past. She lives, she says, "right here and now." The priorities in her life are her family, her creative work with oil paint and knitting, and her friends. "We have a group of fourteen widows who get together and go out to dinner," she says. "It's a lot of go, and a lot of good things happen."

Still, the woman is rooted deeply in her heritage. Her father, Alexis Muriel Charbonneau, was a dispatch carrier for the government in Pierre, South Dakota. He was a descendant of the trapper Charbonneau who accompanied Sacajawea on Lewis and Clark's expedition. "My mother, Jenny Howard, was Lakota and French. She migrated up to Rosebud on the Sioux reservation from southeast Nebraska with her people in the late 1800s. She inherited a ranch in Todd County, an Indian allotment, from her mother." Alexis Charbonneau, a widower with four children, saw opportunity knocking. Todd County was level, flat country, a bit too far east to be in the rolling Sandhills. "There wasn't enough water to support an orchard," Ruby says. "We didn't even have trees around the house. We were just out there, in that wind."

The ranch house was plain with scrubbed, limed floors, with a kitchen big enough for two sets to square dance. "Daddy knew a couple of fiddlers and we had a piano," Ruby recalls. "But I was too young, I always fell asleep." The Charbonneaus had ten more children; each warranted their quarter-section allotment, so the ranch grew to a respectable size. Ruby remembers what a job it was putting up hay.

RUBY STEDRY PHOTO © CAROLYN DUFURRENA. HISTORIC PHOTO COURTESY RUBY STEDRY.

Ruby at age 80, in Nebraska, 1994. INSET: Ruby's father, Alexis Charbonneau, shown here at age sixteen, was a dispatch carrier for the government in Pierre, South Dakota.

"We started right after Fourth of July and tried to get done by Labor Day. Boy, when they put up hay the kids worked. Florence, from the age of fourteen, drove the two-horse stacker team when they were shorthanded. The boys up on the stack would get mad at her for not dropping the hay just right."

They grew all their own produce and had the biggest garden in Todd County. "When Dad went to town to ship cattle, he'd come back with the wagon loaded: four sacks of flour, great big sacks of sugar, coffee in a can that tall, apples in baskets. That would be the winter supply."

Ruby's mother used to feed the hay crews. She had a big cookstove and another cookstove in the bunkhouse that was attached to the house. And she used to have both stoves going. "Susan and Nettie would fry chicken, fry chicken, fry chicken. They would cure hams and bacons, and Mom would can meat. And my dad had a sausage maker. He'd smoke 'em in the smokehouse. Indian turnips came on in June, and Mother would send us out with sharp knives, Zina and me. We'd go looking for a green leaf, gray and fuzzy underneath. We dug it up and ate it like a carrot."

Nettie's quarter section was all corn, which they used for winter feed. "Did you ever eat field corn? Well, it's good when you catch it right, when it's young."

They branded about 75 head of crossbred calves in the spring. Because the land was all fenced, the cattle stayed in pastures until it was grazed down. "But when they got out, they stayed out till the next year. When they'd brand, my mother would say, 'That's no place for young ladies out there.' But we'd sneak up on the barn roof and watch. Zina and I were maybe eleven and eight. We had ponies and we rode the fence lines to see if the fences were up. Except for riding fence and chasing the old gander, we pretty much spent our time at the ranch, up on the barn roof."

In the fall when school would start, Jenny Charbonneau packed her younger children into the buggy and drove 27 miles into Valentine. Her husband and the boys stayed at the ranch all winter. When summertime came, they went back out.

"My mother would take Zina and me across the street in Valentine to the basketball games. Not a one of my brothers played, but my mother loved the game." Ruby spent the winters singing: solos, quartets and glee club. She took two firsts and one second in the Cherry County Singing Contest in sixth grade. And it was in that same class that she met Merit Christopher, her first husband. Tweed knickers, argyle socks, curly blond hair: what dark-eyed country girl could resist?

In the 1920s, the aging Charbonneaus got a couple to stay at the ranch and they moved to town for good. Ruby stayed in Valentine and dressed hair. Some of the older boys stayed at the ranch and helped put up hay, but the allotments were gradually sold as the children moved away and bought places of their own. Ruby held on to her piece, and married her childhood sweetheart after World War II, in 1945. "Merit was in the Air Force. We lived in Grand Island, Denver, Cheyenne, and then Japan." He died in 1954, just ten years into their life together. She came back to the heartland, married feed-mill salesman Frank Stedry, and moved to eastern Nebraska, where she still lives. She still has her piece of the family place.

"My dad didn't want an inch of that land plowed, because it would blow, and he didn't want it ruined. Today it is all native prairie grass." The allotment is rented now to a local rancher.

Ruby wants the land to stay in her family. She has lost her second husband, has no children, and is the sole surviving Charbonneau sibling. But she stays active, selling afghans and oil paintings, seeing friends and her sisters' children, and taking walks. "I am so grateful for my health. I think you have to keep busy, keep your mind functioning. If you sit down in that rocking chair, that rocking chair will get you. So I go, by golly, I go."—*Carolyn Dufurrena*

WYOMING . SUMMER 1994

Earl Lozier, 85

His first paying job was to hold horses for Curl Rungis while he painted them. Rungis was one of the most familiar names around when it came to wildlife painting, and he spent a lot of time at the Box R Ranch with Earl's dad, Irv. "Seemed like I would hold them horses for Rungis for half the day," Earl says. "But boy was I making the money. Twenty-five cents a day!"—*Dan Abernathy*

MONTANA . SUMMER 2004

Don Burke, 81

In 1965, while trailing cows, Don was bucked off a fairly young horse but instead of letting loose, he held on. "I thought my arm was broke. After I finished my job for the day, I went into town to have the doc look at it. He asked me what I did after I was bucked off and I told him, 'I got back on him and rode 'im. What do you think I did?' He looked at me and said that was near impossible because my arm was fine, but my neck was broken."—*Alex Burke*

Don, right, and his cousins ride sheep at the Missouri River Bottom Ranch in 1930.

MONTANA . FALL 1999

Andy Anderson, 82

The unexpected is what you come to expect from Andy Anderson. Small wonder. There aren't too many ranchers in Montana who hold degrees in English literature from prestigious Eastern universities or who have spent months in German prisoner-of-war camps after piloting airplanes that were shot down during World War II.

"That prison camp influenced my thinking," Andy says. "I wanted a quiet life in the country."—*Lee Juillerat*

NEVADA . WINTER 1994

Jack Walther, 74

I am part of this range of waving grass,
Part of the evening breeze, the gentle rains that pass
I am the snows on the mountain that cause the streams to flow,
Spreading out on the valley, urging the grass to grow.
The coyote that howls in the evening or the hoot owl
in the wood,
I sense them stir within my soul. Deep down it feels good.
With this all a part of me, I can never be alone
I am the richest man on earth, for all this I own.

ABANDONED FARM, JORNADA DEL MUERTO, SOCORRO COUNTY, NEW MEXICO. PHOTO © LARRY ANGIER

Santa Fe was America's most cosmopolitan city for centuries before the proud blend of cultures in New Mexico Territory was granted statehood in 1912, recognizing some citizens with ancestors who built and cared for the land at least as long as fellow American families laid claim to New England.

Thelma Weaver, 95, and Ferne Collins, 93

Goshen's first flappers.

Thelma Weaver celebrated her 95th birthday on November 12, 1995, by serving family and friends a well-marbled standing rib roast, Yorkshire pudding, potatoes and gravy—all lovingly prepared in her own kitchen in Goshen, Indiana. The salad and birthday cake were brought by 93-year-old Ferne Collins, Thelma's cousin who lives nearby, and also alone.

Thelma loves cooking. "Corn-fed beef with fat around the edges is best," she says, "but I always eat turkey skin and I love liver and giblets." For a decade in the late 1940s and early '50s, Thelma had a daily radio show called "Cookbook of the Air" on station WLOI in LaPorte, Indiana. Often she had studio audiences and prepared food during the broadcast. "Back then," she says, "there were no meatless meals."

When she had done that long enough, she published a cookbook with recipes donated by her fans. Then she ran for public office. In those days Republicans never won and women never ran. She didn't win either.

PHOTOS COURTESY THELMA WEAVER

FROM TOP: Thelma, left, and Ferne Collins all dressed up for First Communion, 1910. ▪ Horses were always part of the Weaver family. In their later years, Thelma and Buck rode Tennessee Walkers. Rusty is the roan, Sadie is the bay. ▪ Ferne, left, and Thelma today.

As a young mother, Thelma and two friends augmented their family incomes by staging marionette shows in Chicago department stores. They made the puppets themselves and used stage sets they created and painted. In the 1940s, '50s and '60s, Thelma read best sellers and was paid for her dramatic monologues called "book reviews."

Meanwhile, she had a full-time job in a LaPorte bank, the town where she and her family lived for 30 years and she prepared three meals almost every day for her husband, who ate punctually at six, twelve and six. Technically, Thelma and her siblings were orphans because their mother died in 1902 when Thelma was only two years old. They were reared by their grandparents and their large Catholic family.

Thelma and her cousin Ferne were the smallest, and they have remained lifelong friends. In the 1920s, they became two of Goshen's first flappers, scandalizing the family when they bobbed their waist-long tresses and danced the Charleston. Nor did the family approve when Thelma, after high school graduation, took her savings and hopped a train to attend acting school in Chicago.

She ran out of money in less than a year and returned to Goshen and a bank teller's job, but her penchant for drama continued. In 1924, Thelma eloped with Buck Weaver, the man of her dreams. He was 32, eight years older, and boss of the crew that laid bricks on the dirt road in front of her grandfather's house. Buck had been elected county engineer, but in 1932 he lost the job when all Republicans lost elections. By then they had a five-year-old and a brand new baby.

Their Depression stories illustrate Thelma's ability to enjoy life, no matter what. For example: they had moved to a farm where Buck exchanged work for rent. Their ramshackle home had two amenities: a huge, open fireplace and a wood cookstove. She wrote in her diary about a "good day" on that farm when she painted the outhouse a beautiful pink.

Buck had passed the state examination and was a licensed engineer in Indiana, but he had no high school diploma and he clung to politically incorrect ideals. To feed his family, he shot rabbits, squirrels and birds and was not above picking up slices of bread lying in the snow. They survived on odd jobs until 1938 when Buck landed an engineer's job based in LaPorte.

After the children married and he retired, Buck and Thelma bought a small trailer and followed the sun for ten years. Buck died in 1976. Now, Thelma and Ferne go out every day, play bridge at least three times a week and enjoy their many friends. Once a year, they travel to Elko, Nevada, to visit family. There they finance their own entertainment by breaking even at the 21 tables in local casinos. And no matter what they are doing, the "little old ladies" stop for lunch—and you can always bet that it's never a meatless meal.

—*Mary Branscomb*

TEXAS . SPRING 1995

Myrtle Malone, 81

Born when the Texas border was raw and rough.

The folks gathering at the Pumpville Baptist Church for Sunday preaching and community dinner swear Myrtle Malone is the best cook in two counties. Along with bragging on her cooking, they claim she's one of the finest riders in West Texas and say she hasn't missed a roundup in 70 years.

At age 81, she sits straight in the saddle on Julie, her barefooted red mule. With Snow, her border collie, Myrtle and Julie work spring and fall roundups on the family's ranches. "This little mule is more surefooted than a shod horse," she says. "That steep Pecos slickrock gets scary when those shoes start slipping."

The country covered by this spry cowgirl is severe, located on and between the sheer cliffs of the Pecos River and the eroded canyons of the Rio Grande. Twice each year, she covers 80 square miles, herding thousands of Angora goats and Rambouillet sheep into shearing pens. "I love it!" Myrtle says. "Out there I can talk to God, just Him and me. A couple of hours in the saddle and all my cares and troubles fall away."

Her roots grow deep in the empty lands between the rivers. In 1895, her maternal grandparents, William Issac and Laura Alice Babb, homesteaded several sections near Pandale. It was a hard day's ride from Langtry, Texas. After years of ranching, they moved to Langtry and eventually owned all the property between there and Pandale, including Judge Roy Bean's Jersey Lily Saloon. Laura Alice wanted to tear the saloon down and use the lumber on a barn, but William believed sightseers might be interested one day, so they left it alone. In 1935 the family donated the saloon to the state of Texas and it now sits on the grounds of the Judge Roy Bean Visitor Center in Langtry.

Myrtle's father, Shannon Stapp, was the great-grandson of Elijah Stapp, a signer of the Texas Declaration of Independence. He moved to Val Verde County in 1907 to drill the first water well and erect an Eclipse windmill on the Babb headquarters ranch. He met and married William Babb's daughter, Rosa Ellen, and they immediately filed a claim on land above Fielder Draw, west of the Pecos River.

PHOTO COURTESY R.W. BANHAGEL

Myrtle and Julie the mule ride the tough West Texas terrain to round up the herd. Myrtle ranks high in both cooking and riding among her friends.

Myrtle was born in Langtry when the border was raw and rough, but she grew up on the homestead. The family lived with their Angoras because of predators. "When I was five, I remember my mother riding out to tend the goats, taking a baby on a pillow in front of her and one or two of us behind. She'd carry kid goats in gunnysacks hanging from the saddle horn. This was done during the years when goats were being herded on land without fences. The nannies were driven to large pens late in the evening and all the new kids were tied by the foot to a stake, while my mother brought the correct nanny to the kid for the night."

Education was hard to come by. Schools were days away and the children were needed on the ranch, so Shannon and Rosa hired governesses to live with the family and tutor the five children. "My sister Maude and I pulled pranks on them all the time," Myrtle says. "We hoped if we scared them bad enough they'd quit. Once we put a dead bull snake just inside the outhouse door so the teacher would see it when she sat down. Another time we stuck a dead skunk by the door."

In later years, Myrtle attended high school 180 miles from the ranch in Alpine, Texas. She boarded there and traveled by bus to be home on holidays. She was always proud of her family heritage, and says, "We Babbs are tough!" It is a fact that the family is part of Texas ranching history: fighting through years of floods, poverty and drought, years marked by hundreds of roundups and thousands of hours in the saddle, years of living miles from neighbors and towns at the end of a faint dirt trail.

"We ate what we grew or hunted, fresh vegetables from our garden, beef, venison, lamb and young goat," Myrtle recalls. "That good food gave me the strength to work hard all these years. I'm thankful to the Lord for my health, many blessings, and for the years of my life. I know I can do nothing without the Lord."—*J. Zane Walley*

CALIFORNIA . SUMMER 2008

Frank Long, 82

"It takes a lot more land than I have to make a living off cattle in these parts," says Frank Long, talking about the economics of raising beef in California's Sierra foothills. "That's why we've grabbed other opportunities as they came along." He gives some examples: "Raising oat hay, cutting firewood, selling granite boulders and staging Civil War battle reenactments. We keep busy." Frank was raised on ranches in the foothills east of Fresno where the family raised cattle and grain. "It was a hardscrabble life," he says. "We didn't have electricity or a phone until after I graduated from high school in 1943."—*Virgil Mullis*

NEVADA . SPRING 2008

Jess Sustacha, 85

He was born in the beautiful Lamoille valley about twenty miles south of Elko, Nevada. And he's spent 85 years beneath the Ruby Mountains, sometimes likened to the Swiss Alps for their rugged and unforgiving beauty.

Jess Sustacha is only one generation removed from the Basque country. His parents, Jose Sustacha (born in Bilbao, Spain, in 1887) and Francisca Arambarri (born in Berriatus, Viscaya, in 1891), immigrated separately from the Basque country in Spain; he in 1910, she in 1913. They met and married in 1916 in Elko while Jose worked for Pete Garat on the Spanish Ranch near Tuscarora, and she worked in a Basque-owned hotel in Elko.

Jose's ranch was divided between Jess and Joe in 1966. "The water rights on the whole ranch are the oldest and the best in the valley," Jess says. "Some were established in the 1800s. We have willows for shelter—important during calving—and plenty of natural meadows so we don't have to be farming all the time." Hereford cattle have been raised by the Sustacha family for more than 100 years. The first were acquired from the University of Nevada, Reno, which had imported them from England.

Jess always loved his animals. "Peppy is the best horse I've ever ridden—a sorrel with a white stripe down his face—an excellent cow horse. All I have to do is spur and hang on. I really treat him good and he takes good care of me." His favorite dog was Bozo, a blue heeler, "a one-person dog. He would ride with me in the front seat and when we went to town, I'd stop and buy him a vanilla ice cream cone. When we were out riding, he'd catch a cottontail and put his paw on it to hold it down until we went by with the cattle. Then he would turn the bunny loose. You could tell him to stay in a gate and he would be there forever. Sometimes I would forget him and have to go back with the pickup to get him."—*Mary Branscomb*

COLORADO . SPRING 2008

John Robertson, 85

"As a young boy, my job was to fetch wood for the cook-stove and heating stove. I was riding horses and roping by the time I was six or seven. This wasn't unusual as most of the boys in this country worked as soon as they were big enough to straddle a horse. By the time I was a teenager, I was pretty good at it."

He continues: "Some might think this country is bare and desolate with nothin' but cactus, prairie dogs and cedar trees, but on a clear night you can almost touch the stars. To me, the howl of a coyote at a full moon is better music than an opera."

When John's parents came to Colorado, they came in a covered wagon from Foard County, Texas. "I wish I had paid more attention when they talked about it. A lot has changed since the women wore sunbonnets and kept house in a dugout with a dirt floor."

John joined the Navy to see the world. "It made me realize there is no place like Colorado."

—*Connie Vigil Platt*

NEVADA . FALL/WINTER 1992

Loyd Sorensen, 92

Dealing with government agents has been a way of life for Loyd since the Taylor Grazing Act was passed in 1936. Because he and his late wife, Alta Hinton, made their living as newlyweds by tending sheep on public range, the Taylor Grazing Act put them out of business. However, Loyd does not resent the act itself. "It stabilized the industry," he explains. "It cleaned out the people who weren't paying their way. I was one of 'em."

In the 1950s there were only four BLM and five U.S. Forest Service employees in Elko. "One reason I built a home in town was to keep an eye on them," Loyd says. "Those nine people used to help ranchers build roads and fences. Now you can't count 'em all. And there's less range work being done."

In 1991, the BLM in Elko reported 74 employees and the Forest Service had 83.—*Mary Branscomb*

The Hans C. Sorensen family in front of their home in Mt. Carmel, Utah. Loyd is fourth from the left in front of his father. His sisters, Marie and Vilage, are in front of the fence. The other people in the photo are members of the Englestead family.

ILLINOIS . WINTER 2009

Hank Klunk, 94

The Klunk hog farm is located on a sharp curve along a busy highway. "People didn't go so fast before they paved the road, but now they don't slow down for anything," Hank says. "I can't tell you how many cars have missed the curve and wound up in the hog lot. I'd have to get out in the middle of the night and deal with hogs running loose and a fence down. If you have ever dug a fence post hole in frozen ground, you know it isn't easy."—*Joyce Morrison*

OREGON . WINTER 2002

Ray Blasingame, 83

Riding snorty bucking horses can be pretty intimidating, but for Ray Blasingame it was a great job. "It was fun because nobody was shooting at you," he chuckles.

If riding wild horses seemed fun, it's because Ray spent several years as an Army paratrooper during World War II. A member of the 101st Airborne Division, he was among the 6,000 men who parachuted behind German lines during the predawn hours on D-day at Omaha Beach in occupied France. "I wasn't afraid to take chances," he explains. That's why he volunteered for the paratroopers—that and the fact it paid an extra $100 a month.

Ray has often taken chances. He was born 83 years ago in the South Dakota town of Timber Lake. He took a chance in 1940 when he was 21 and moved to Oregon. "The reason I came was I had heard of the ZX Ranch. I heard they had enough horses to keep a person busy."

Ray was more than busy riding wild horses that had been raised on the open range. His job was to gentle them enough so they could be used by ZX cowboys. "When I came here they were running 30,000 head of cattle. They had twenty cowboys with a chuck wagon. The ZX Ranch (then the Chewaucan Land & Cattle Company) was one of the biggest in the Northwest. It was interesting work for me and that's why I did it. It provided a challenge."—*Lee Juillerat*

PHOTO © LARRY ANGIER

Tom Oneto, 80-something, is a third-generation rancher whose grandparents immigrated from Italy in the late 1800s. He's talking ranching with fourth-generation cowboy, Doug Joses, during an Independence Day celebration. They are at the Cuneo Ranch cabin, which is on deeded land in Blue Creek Canyon in the Stanislaus National Forest of Calaveras County, California. Doug and his wife Loree raise cattle, cater cattle sales and cowboy weddings, and cook at family gatherings.